D1568813

LEONEL RUGAMA

THE EARTH IS A SATELLITE OF THE MOON

translated by
Sara Miles
Richard Schaaf
Nancy Weisberg

CURBSTONE PRESS

First edition: León, ediciones Taller, © l978
Second edition: La Habana, Casa de las Américas, © l983

© Leonel Rugama.
© 1984 Editorial Nueva Nicaragua, 3rd edition.
translation © 1985 Sara Miles, Richard Schaaf, Nancy Weisberg.
All Rights Reserved.

Our deepest thanks to those who helped make this book possible:

Solomón Alarcón
Lisandro Chavez
Instituto por el Estudio de Sandinismo
Juan José Godoy
Flor de María Monterrey
Margaret Randall
Arlene Scully
James Scully
and to Comandante Omar Cabezas, Comandante Doris Tijerino,
and Doña Candida Rugama for their contributions.

cover photo: Brian Ruonavaara

THE HOUSES WERE STILL FULL OF SMOKE first appeared in ALCA-
TRAZ, spring 1985. "I am René Espronceda de la Barca" first appeared in
FICTION INTERNATIONAL, fall, 1985.

**This book was produced with the support of
The Connecticut Commission on the Arts
The National Endowment for the Arts**

**LC 85-62201
ISBN 0-915306-50-6 (paper)
ISBN 0-915306-54-9 (cloth)**

**CURBSTONE PRESS
321 Jackson Street
Willimantic, CT
06226
USA**

THE EARTH IS A SATELLITE OF THE MOON

EPITAFIO

Leonel Rugama
gozó de la tierra prometida
en el mes más crudo de la siembra
sin más alternativa que la lucha,
muy cerca de la muerte,
pero no del final.

—1970

EPITAPH

· Leonel Rugama
rejoiced in the promised land
in the hardest month of the planting
with no choice but the struggle
very near death
but nowhere near
the end.

—1970

LA TIERRA ES UN SATÉLITE DE LA LUNA

El Apolo 2 costó más que el Apolo 1
el Apolo 1 costó bastante.

El Apolo 3 costó más que el Apolo 2
el Apolo 2 costó más que el Apolo 1
el Apolo 1 costó bastante.

El Apolo 4 costó más que el Apolo 3
el Apolo 3 costó más que el Apolo 2
el Apolo 2 costó más que el Apolo 1
el Apolo 1 costó bastante.

El Apolo 8 costó un montón, pero no se sintió
porque los astronautas eran protestantes
y desde la luna leyeron la Biblia,
maravillando y alegrando a todos los cristianos
y a la venida el papa Paulo VI les dio la bendición.

El Apolo 9 costó más que todos juntos
junto con el Apolo 1 que costó bastante.

Los bisabuelos de la gente de Acahualinca tenían menos
     hambre que los abuelos.
Los bisabuelos se murieron de hambre.
Los abuelos de la gente de Acahualinca tenían menos
     hambre que los padres.
Los abuelos murieron de hambre.
Los padres de la gente de Acahualinca tenían menos
     hambre que los hijos de la gente de allí.
Los padres se murieron de hambre.

THE EARTH IS A SATELLITE OF THE MOON

Apollo 2 cost more than Apollo 1
Apollo 1 cost plenty.

Apollo 3 cost more than Apollo 2
Apollo 2 cost more than Apollo 1
Apollo 1 cost plenty.

Apollo 4 cost more than Apollo 3
Apollo 3 cost more than Apollo 2
Apollo 2 cost more than Apollo 1
Apollo 1 cost plenty.

Apollo 8 cost a fortune, but no one minded
because the astronauts were Protestant
they read the Bible from the moon
astounding and delighting every Christian
and on their return Pope Paul VI gave them his blessing.

Apollo 9 cost more than all these put together
including Apollo 1 which cost plenty.

The great-grandparents of the people of Acahaulinca were less
        hungry than the grandparents.
The great-grandparents died of hunger.
The grandparents of the people of Acahaulinca were less
        hungry than the parents.
The grandparents died of hunger.
The parents of the people of Acahaulinca were less
        hungry than the children of the people there.
The parents died of hunger.

La gente de Acahualinca tiene menos hambre que los hijos
   de la gente de allí.
Los hijos de la gente de Acahualinca no nacen por hambre,
   y tienen hambre de nacer, para morirse de hambre.
Bienaventurados los pobres porque de ellos será la luna.

The people of Acahaulinca are less hungry than the children
     of the people there.
The children of the people of Acahaulinca, because of hunger,
     are not born
they hunger to be born, only to die of hunger.
Blessed are the poor for they shall inherit the moon.

O JUGAR AJEDREZ

1.

A principios de 1968
cuando yo no había ajustado los diecinueve años
y llegaba a jugar ajedrez
todas las tardes a la casa de Carlitos Argeñal
y toda la tarde jugando
     y cuando salía
salía embotado de tanto pensar
     y él me preguntaba
que si iba a volver mañana
     y yo le decía que sí
     y siempre le decía que sí
menos los sábados
porque su hermana se andaba peinando
y a él le tocaba cuidar la venta
     y tampoco los domingos
porque su hermana se alistaba
    en la mañana
para ir a la misa de diez
     y en la tarde
para ir al cine.

2.

Cuando jugábamos él me ganaba
       y me ganaba
       y me ganaba
hasta que salía embotado
pero siempre me decía
      que yo tenía madera

O TO PLAY CHESS

1.

Early in 1968
when I hadn't turned nineteen yet
I started playing chess
every afternoon at Carlitos Argeñal's house
playing all afternoon
                          and when I'd leave
I'd leave numb from thinking so much
                          and he would ask me
if I was going to come back tomorrow
                          and I'd say yes
                          I would always say yes
except Saturdays
because his sister went to have her hair done
and it was his turn to look after the store
                          and also not on Sundays
because his sister had to get herself ready
                          in the morning
to go to ten o'clock Mass
                          and in the afternoon
to go to the movies.

2.

When we played he used to beat me
                          and beat me
                                    and beat me
until I'd leave numb
but he always said
                    I had potential

y que él me ganaba por la experiencia
y que cuando él empezó
                    siempre le ganaban
                        y le ganaban
                            y que era peor
porque don Milcíades después que le ganaba
                    se ponía a burlarse
y le decía que nunca le iba a ganar.
Pasamos varios meses jugando
                    en su casa
y en un tablerito
donde colocábamos unas grandes piezas de otro ajedrez
y Carlitos siempre decía
                    que el tablero de esas piezas
era con todo y mesa
                        y era de los buenos
porque los cuadros no eran pintados
                    sino incrustrados en la mesa
                        (y eso era lo mejor)
pero que no jugábamos en ella
                    porque estaba ocupada
con un montón de chunches
                        y calachero de la venta
y era mejor jugar en ese tablerito.

3.

Un día le llegó una carta
                    del club de ajedrez de Masaya
y le decían que ellos ya estaban organizados
que la carta se la dirigían a él
                            por considerarlo
el jugador más energético de esa región.

that he beat me with his experience
that when he'd first started
                        they always beat him
                                    and beat him
                                    and *that* was worse
because after don Milcíades beat him
                        he'd rub it in
and tell him he was never going to win.
We spent months playing
                        in his house
on a small chessboard
where we set up some enormous pieces from a different chess set
and Carlitos would always say
                        that the chessboard to those pieces
was a table and all
                        that it was one of the best
because the squares instead of being painted on
                        were inlaid
                        (and that was better)
but that we weren't playing on it
                        because it was covered
with a whole bunch of stuff
                        odds & ends from the store
so it was better to play on this small chessboard.

3.

One day he received a letter
                        from the chess club in Masaya
they said that they were now organized
that they had addressed the letter to him
                        considering him
the most enthusiastic player in the region.

17

Entonces empezamos a organizar el club
fuimos a conseguir unas mesas
                            de un club que se había desintegrado
y sólo conseguimos una
                    y toda mantecosa
                            y llena de groña
con los cantos como mordidos
y Carlitos dijo:
"por cuentas aquí abrían las chibolas"
                        conseguimos una casa
y allí nos poníamos a jugar toda la tarde
y allí llegaba don Constantino
                    y Fermín y Moncho
pero llegábamos más
don Constantino, Carlitos, y yo
y allí pasábamos toda la tarde jugando.

4.

Peón rey cuatro rey (PR4R)
peón rey cuatro rey (PR4R)
alfil rey cuatro alfil (AR4A)
caballo dama tres alfil (CD3A)
                        (protegiendo su peón central)
caballo dama tres alfil (CD3A)
                        (protegiendo su peón central)
alfil rey cuatro alfil (AR4A)
                        (desarrollándose)
caballo rey tres alfil (CR3A)
                (atacando peón central defendido por el caballo)
la apertura siempre era rápida
                  y en silencio
después ya se empezaba
                  dele dele hasta que se le pele

Then we began to organize
we went to get some tables
                    from a club which had broken up
but we only got one
                    and it was all greasy
                            and it squeaked
and its edges were all chewed up
and Carlitos said:
"it looks like they used to crack marbles on it"
                    we found a house
and there we started playing every afternoon
and there don Constantino
                    and Fermin and Moncho came
but mostly
don Constantino, Carlitos, and me
and there we spent every afternoon playing.

4.

King's pawn to king four (KP4K)
King's pawn to king four (KP4K)
King's bishop to bishop four (KB4B)
Queen's knight to bishop three (QB3B)
                    (protecting his center pawn)
Queen's knight to bishop three (QB3B)
                    (protecting his center pawn)
King's bishop to bishop four (KB4B)
                    (developing)
King's knight to bishop three (KK3B)
                    (attacking center pawn defended by the knight)
the opening always went quickly
in silence
then it would begin:
                    hit him hit him hit him till he's exposed

19

cuando uno hacía una buena jugada
                    Carlitos tomaba la pieza
                    y lentamente la movía
haciendo una mejor
                    y diciendo:
"aquí no se le permitirán libertades"
                    o la bebe
                    o la derrama
y jaque
        jaque
                jaque
amigó, aquí un error se paga con sangre
amigó, aquí un error se paga con sangre
amigó, aquí un error se paga con sangre
amigó, aquí un error se paga con sangre
                            y quedaba repitiéndola
                            y repitiéndola
mientras pensaba la combinación
                            y al rato
caballo siete dama (C7D)
                            y yo quedaba diciendo
bueeno, bueeno, bueeno, bueeno
bueeno, bueeno, bueeeeno, bueeeeeeeeno
ajá?
y moviendo y moviendo y moviendo
la pierna
        como temblando
                    y el zapato como chillando
bueeeee, bueeeno, bueeeeee, bueeeeeeeeeeeeno
                    y el zapato como chillando
mientras pensaba la contestación.
O
don Tino

when you made a good move
                    Carlitos would take his piece
                    and slowly move it
making a better one
                    saying
"here no liberties will be permitted"
                              you swallow it
                              or you bleed to death
and check
          check
                    check
friend, here you paid for a mistake with blood
friend, here you paid for a mistake with blood
friend, here you paid for a mistake with blood
friend, here you paid for a mistake with blood
                                   he kept repeating it
                                   and repeating it
meanwhile thinking out the series of moves
                                   and in a little while
Knight to queen seven (K7Q)
                         and I kept saying
goood, goood, goooood, goood
goood, goood, gooooooood, gooooooooooood
uh-huh?
and moving and moving and moving
my leg
       as if it were trembling
                    and my shoe as if it were screeching
goooo, gooooood, goooooo, gooooooooooood
                    and my shoe as if it were screeching
while he was thinking of a response.
O
don Tino

Ah? Carlitos ah? Carlitos
Ah? ah? Ah?
Carlitos tos Tostos tos tostos
que f-e-o la m-e-t-e ah?
y después jugaba
                    y después
jaque
atiéndame el jaquecito por favor
y jaque con caballo seis alfil rey (+C6AR)
atiéndame el jaquecito por favor (don Tinito)
es que mis caballos patean duro
                    y por último
jaque
      jaque
            jaque
jaque mate (+ +).

5.

Casi siempre ganaba Carlitos
pero algunas veces que le ganábamos
                    salía preocupado
y decía que no estaba nítido
                    o que le molestaban las amebas
                    o que no había almorzado
y contaba que a los grandes campeones rusos
les llevaban hasta sus mujeres
para que no estuvieran pensando
y decía que el ajedrez era un juego delicado
                    y si no se estaba nítido se perdía.

uh-huh Carlitos? uh Carlitos
uh-huh
Carlitos (cough coughcoughcough)
t-w-i-s-t it in
                        uh-huh?
and then he moved
                    then
check
you're in check
check, knight to king's bishop six (+ K6KB)
you're in check (don Tinito)
you see my knights fight back hard
                                and at last
check
        check
                check
checkmate (+ +).

5.

Carlitos almost never lost
but the few times we beat him
                    he would leave, beside himself
saying he wasn't sharp
                    or wasn't feeling so good
                    or hadn't eaten any lunch
he'd be going on about the great Russian champions
who even brought their wives
so their thoughts wouldn't wander off
he was saying chess was a delicate game
                    if you weren't sharp, you lost.

6.

Por el club siempre pasaba una muchacha
pero por la acera de enfrente
la misma muchacha a la que le he dedicado varios poemas
a la que me quedaba "ido en clase viéndole las piernas"
                              (de otro poema)
y todas las tardes pasaba de clase
                              y yo estaba en el club jugando
                                    o viendo jugar
y ella me dijo una vez
                              que siempre pasaba
y que yo no le hacía caso
despuúes la busqué
                y dejé de ir al club
y dejé el ajedrez
("y si no se estaba nítido se perdía")
y por el ajedrez había dejado el fútbol.
Entonces yo andaba en los diecinueve años
e iba a cumplir los veinte.

6.

A girl always walked by the club
(but always across the street)
the same girl I'd dedicated several poems to
the one who left me "dazed in class looking at her legs"
                              (from another poem)
and every afternoon she walked by from class
                              and I'd be in the club playing
                              or watching
and one time she told me
                    she always walked by
and that I paid no attention to her.
After that, I looked for her
                    and I stopped going to the club
I quit chess
("if you weren't sharp, you lost")
just like I quit soccer for chess.
By then I was nineteen
going on twenty.

JUEGOS

Allí siempre había muchachos jugando.
En abril, mayo y junio
jugaban chibolas
        o canicas
             o maules.
Jugaban hasta de a cuarenta
hacían ruedotas
        colocaban chibolas
                rojas
                    amarillas
                        verdes
rojas amarillas y verdes
rojas con amarillo y verde
claras. oscuras, tiernas
           olivo
         marino
              celeste.
El punto bien largo
          ' y antes de tirar
latigándose con el índice
entre el pulgar y el corazón
para probarse el pulso.
        El sol como inmenso chibolón amarillo
        caía quemando la rueda del horizonte.
Toda la tarde:
        sonando chibolas
        ganando chibolas
        perdiendo chibolas
        comprando chibolas
        vendiendo chibolas

GAMES

There were always kids playing over there.
In April, May and June
they used to play marbles
                shooting marbles
                        or doing tricks with marbles.
As many as forty played
in big circles
                arranging their marbles
                        reds
                           yellows
                               greens
reddish-yellows and greens
yellowish-green reds
clear ones, dark ones, mediums
                    olives
                      sea-greens
                             heavenly blues
The mark was pretty far
                and before shooting
they kept flicking their index finger
between the thumb and the middle finger
to steady their wrist.
                The sun like an immense yellow marble
                fell burning into the circle of the horizon.
All afternoon long:
                blowing on marbles
                winning marbles
                losing marbles
                buying marbles
                selling marbles

              chocando chibolas
              quebrando chibolas.
Fijándonos que mida bien la cuarta
                      que no meta puya
                            o yanka
viendo si cae orca.
Enrollándose en el suelo
escupiendo los dedos
              frotando la chibola para tirar
poniéndonos en rueda
          juntos
             sobre-juntos
tirando de punto.
Poniéndonos macho muerto
apartándonos de los carros
              y los camiones de don Aníbal.
Cuidando las chibolas
discutiendo por chibolas
arrebatando chibolas
llorando por chibolas.
              Hasta que se encendían las bujías
                  nos íbamos a casa
                      yo llegaba con miedo
                      y las tortillas frías.
Valencia 50
          Montecarlo 20
              Esfinge 100
                 Polar 1000
(en toda Nicaragua los extranjeros valen 1000)
o en cualquier acera.

                    jiggling marbles
                    breaking marbles
We figured it was well worth the whip
                              but not the machete tip
                                        nor the rack
to stay to see if the killer whale marble would bite the dust.
Maneuvering around in the dirt
spitting on our fingers
                        rubbing the marble
                        getting ready to shoot
we formed a circle
                all together
                close together
                        on top of each other
shooting the mark.
We were becoming tough guys
far away from the cars
                    and trucks
                            of don Aníbal.
Guarding marbles
arguing over marbles
snatching away marbles
crying over marbles.
                    Until they lit the streetlamps
                    and we'd go home
                    I'd go in scared
                            with the cold tortillas.
Valencia 50
          Montecarlo 20
                    Sphinx 100
                              Polar 1000
(all over Nicaragua the foreigners are worth 1000)
or on any sidewalk.

                    Jugábamos tabas en las esquinas
                    todo el mes de junio
                         de agosto
                             y de septiembre.
Cogiendo la taba
          y tirando la taba,
                    cogiendo la taba. . .
Los perros pasaban a mear los postes de luz.
Aparecían personas
             desaparecían personas
             hablaban del trabajo
             preguntando la hora
                    riéndose
                         hablando
                             perdiéndose
                                 doblando las esquinas.
Un hombre serio sobre un caballo
dando saltitos
tronando los cascos
levantando la cola
y dejando una fila de cagajones
                         olorosos
                             húmedos
                                 humeantes.
Sentados en la acera
             pintando culo
                    y cayendo carne
limpiando en ladrillo.
Culo, culo, culo,
          dan ganas de pelear,
(con carne se gana, con culo se pierde)
con pinina
          o panameña se gana doble.

We played knucklebones on streetcorners
all of June
                August
                        and September.
Picking up knucklebones
                throwing down knucklebones
                                picking up knucklebones. . .
Dogs would pass, pissing on lampposts.
People appeared
                disappeared
                talking about work
                asking the time
                        laughing
                                chatting
                                        getting lost
                                                turning corners.
One dignified looking gent went by on his horse
it kicked up
clattered its hooves
raised its tail
leaving behind a trail of
                foul
                        damp
                                steaming horseshit.
Sitting on the sidewalk
                hoping for flats
                        but only turning up knucks
we were cleaned out.
Flats, flats, flats
                it made us feel like fighting
(with knucks you won, with flats you lost)
with *pininas*
                or Panamanians you won double.

La taba en mi casa siempre caía
                              culo
con las tortillas tarde.
Para octubre y noviembre
se hacían remolinos de viento
con pedacitos de zacate seco y tierra
                    y decían que era el diablo
                    y hacían cruces de cenizas.
Los muchachos elevaban lechuzas
                y siempre me quedaba viéndolas
estaban lejos
                y los zopilotes les pasaban cerca.
Unos le echaban hasta cinco rollos de hilo.
Entre los remolinos de la placita
estábamos los grupos de muchachos
y unos jalando el hilo casi hasta los ojos
                y dejándolo ir
        jalando casi hasta los ojos
                y dejándolo ir. . .
la lechuza se mecía suave
                y se perdía cada vez más.
Todos los grupos caminando retrocediendo,
                caminando retrocediendo,
entre los remolinos de viento y tierra
parecíamos Bolívar cruzando los Andes
como sale en las películas
                        o en los cuentos.
Por este tiempo también llegaban los circos
con caballos y monos
                y perros
                        y
                cabras
y varias muchachas que me gustaban

In my house the knucklebones always landed
                              flats
along with the cold tortillas.
Toward October and November
blustering winds were blowing
bits of straw and dirt all over the place
                    and folks were saying it was the devil
                    and crossing themselves with ashes.
The boys flew owl-kites
                    and always I'd hang around watching them
they were so far off
                    turkey-buzzards would circle around them.
Some kids let out five spools of kitestring.
Our gang used to fly kites in the square
where it was always blowing up a storm
tugging the twine almost to our eyes
                    and letting it go
             tugging it almost to our eyes
                    then letting it go. . .
the kites swayed gently side to side
                    each time giving way more and more. . .
Everyone was backstepping
             backstepping
amidst the swirling gusts and the dirt
we looked like Bolívar crossing the Andes
like in the movies
             or in the storybooks.
Around this time also the circus came
with horses and monkeys
                    dogs
                and
                goats
and some girls that I liked

porque en la noche salían casi desnudas dentro del circo.
Nos reuníamos un montón de muchachos
para ver a los hombres abriendo los hoyos
y preguntarles si venían de Honduras
y si hoy en la noche darían función
                                y que cuánto valía
después les tirábamos piedras a los animales
                        y nos colgamos de los tubos
hasta que los dueños nos corrían.
Llegaba alegre contando lo del circo
                        en mi casa siempre serios
me cogían las tortillas-heladas.
En diciembre
las dueñas de cantinas
construían chinamos en la placita
                cubrían todo el suelo con aserrín.
Allí llegaban putas de toda Nicaragua
                        vendedoras de Managua
                                jugadoras de dado
                                        toro rabón
ruletas grandes y pequeñas.
Hacían una barrera
que echaba tufo a berrinche y mierda de gente
y el corralillo de toros
                        a crin de buey y mierda de vaca
(en la barrera se cagaban las vendedoras de Managua)
frente a la barrera de noche
se ponen las poncheras
"La tinaja sobre el tizón
        la mujer enrollada en la toalla"
soplando el tizón debajo de la tinaja Edwin Yllescas.
En la tarde cuando pasaba por la placita
a traer las tortillas donde doña Foncha

34

because at night they came out almost naked in the circus.
A bunch of us kids got together
to watch the men putting up the tents
asking them if they came from Honduras
and if they were going to give a show tonight
                        and how much would it cost
later on we threw stones at the animals
                        and hung from the tentpoles
until the bosses came and chased us away.
And I'd arrive in high spirits talking about the circus
                        in my always solemn house
and get yelled at for the ice-cold tortillas.
In December
the bar owners
built fair-booths in the square
                        and covered the grounds with sawdust.
Whores from all over Nicaragua showed up
                        peddlers from Managua
                                crap shooters
                                    con artists
big time roulette players and small fry.
They made a pit
that gave off the ornery stench of human shit
and a little bullfighting ring
                        full of oxhair and cowshit
(the peddlers from Managua were shitting in the pit)
and at night the women who sell hot punch
set themselves up across from the pit
"The earthen jar on the coals
            the woman wrapped up in the towel"
blowing on the coals under the earthen jar (Edwin Yllescas).
In the afternoon when I went by the square
to get tortillas from doña Foncha

35

me quedaba en la placita jugando
y allí me encontraba con mi tío Heriberto
                    y siempre andaba bolo
                    y una vez lo echaron preso
porque gritó: VIVA AGUADO.
Y lo pusieron a arrancar espinas en el parque
y mi abuela fue a hablar con el comandante
"Dele un rifle para que se vaya a la montaña"
le dijo el comandante.
Mi abuelita le dijo que su hijo no tenía
instintos criminales
y que si los tuviera
ya se hubiera metido a la guardia.
Yo jugaba al siete mayor
con dados rojos grandes y puntitos negros.
Hay veces jugaba toro-rabón
                    tirando la chibola fuerte para que girara
                    por todos los números
en las ruletas no jugaba porque mucho roban.
Hasta que llegaban de mi casa
                    para que llevara las tortillas.

                                        1968/1969

I'd hang around in the square playing
and there I'd run into uncle Heriberto
                    who was always going around drunk
                    and one time they threw him in jail
because he was yelling: VIVA AGUADO.
They put him to work uprooting brambles in the park
and my grandmother went to talk with the captain of the Guard
"Give him a rifle so he can go to the mountains,"
the captain told her.
And my grandmother told him that her son didn't have
criminal instincts
and if he did have them
he'd already have joined the National Guard.
I played craps
with big red dice with little black dots.
Sometimes the con artist played with us
                    throwing the dice spinning them hard
                    shooting the works
but he would never play roulette because they robbed you blind.
Until they came from home
          looking for me
                    and for the tortillas.

1968/1969

TERMINAR TRASTORNÁNDOSE

Mi tío era de raza alta
pero más que su estatura
recuerdo sus botas ticas
                    bien adelgazadas
los dobleces llenos de polvo
y el resto con brillo de ladrillo viejo.
                    Abrochadas por detrás
con hebillas bellísimas
                    antiguas
                    amarillas
                    opacas
                    de bronce.
Nunca le vi los pies desnudos
pero estoy seguro que eran claros
                    claros porosos
y llenos de venas brotadas—no azuladas—.
                    Las uñas alargadas amarillentas
                    y llenas de líneas.
Con su olor seco de tela.
El pantalón de dril
                    vertical
no era limpísimo
            y siempre parecía lleno de polvo--pero parejo--
que contrastaba maravillosamente con cualquier día nublado.
Con todos sus hábitos
                    de tomar mejorales en exceso
                    ponerse una visera
cuando entraba el sol amarillo
por la puerta del corredor
mientras él sorgetaba.

ENDING UP ALL SCREWED UP

My uncle was from a good family
but more than his stature
I remember his Costa Rican boots
                                        elegantly tapered
shining with the lustre of old ceramic tile
except for the cracks filled with dust.
                                    They fastened in the back
with beautiful
            antique
            gilded
            dark
            bronze buckles.
I never saw his bare feet
but I'm sure they were pale
                        porous pale
full of bulging (not blue) veins
                and with long yellowish toenails
                covered with hairline cracks
Smelling of musty cloth.
His long
            bluejeans
weren't the cleanest
            they always seemed covered with dust—but evenly—
which made a marvelous contrast to any cloudy day!
Along with his habit
                    of taking too many aspirins
                    he would put on a visor
whenever the sun came shining
through the doorway into the hall
while he soaked it up.

Una visera tostada
de plástico verde
            mantecosa
            opacada de sudor
                        y de tierra
                                    y de vieja.
Comer con un tenedor de plata
y en plato de china
                  de los de antes.
Ya oscuro ponerse a caminar
                  para un lado
                  y para otro en la sala
después irse a los billares
a ver jugar
            o jugar carambola
                  o pool
                        o quién sabe qué.
Y antes de llegar a la casa
echarse un trago de a peso
y salir chupándose media naranja agria.
Antes de dormirse leer
                  hasta altas horas de la noche
sólo con un foco (cuando sabía que eso era malo para la vista
                  y para la cabeza).
Leía *Selecciones*
          y novelas de guerra
de unas que en la pasta salen aviones en picada
o de aventuras como:
PERDIDO POR LAS ALTAS SELVAS DE BORNEO
ilustrada con gorilas que se robaban a las mujeres.
Siempre que pasaba yo con el candil

A tan visor
with green plastic
                all greasy
                and stained with sweat
                                dirt
                                        and age.
He used to eat with a silver fork
on a china plate
                like in the old days.
And as soon as it got dark
                he would start to pace
                                back and forth
                                in the living room.
Later, he would go down to the pool hall
to watch
        or play billiards
                        or pool
                                or whatever.
And before coming home
he would have a strong drink
and leave, sucking on a bitter orange half.
Before falling asleep he read
                        until all hours of the night
by only a single lightbulb
                        (though he knew it was bad for his eyes
                        and gave him a headache besides).
He read the *Digest*
                and war novels
with guys on the cover flying dive-bombers
or adventure stories like:
LOST IN THE HIGH JUNGLES OF BORNEO
illustrated with pictures of gorillas abducting women.
When I would go with the oil-lamp

a orinar en el patio antes de acostarme
él estaba leyendo
       y cuando pasaba a la vuelta
       y le decía que pasara buenas noches
él seguía ingrido leyendo.
Había veces que mi abuela pasaba a media noche
       por cualquier retorcijón
       o cualquier necesidad
       o a correr los gatos
            para que no botaran los cumbos
y contaba que mi tío estaba leyendo.
       Y seguir tomando exceso de mejorales.
       Y seguir leyendo hasta altas horas de la noche
era un desmando
       y falta de consideración
e
iba a terminar trastornándose decía mi abuela.
Gozaba de una barba cafesosa
       cerrada
          y picoteada de canas
de una gran frente
       y nariz aguileña
canas suaves
siempre apelmasadas hacia atrás.

Ahorita que encontré en un cajón
el tomo casi disuelto
       y sin forro de:
PERDIDO POR LAS ALTAS SELVAS DE BORNEO
me acordé que hace bastante mi tío
se perdio.

                        to pee in the courtyard
                        before going to bed
he'd be reading
                and on the way back
                I'd wish him goodnight
and he'd just go on wrapped up in his reading.
There were times my grandmother got up at midnight
                because of cramps
                or some other necessity
                or to chase the cats away
                        so they wouldn't knock the gourds around
and she'd check to see if my uncle was still reading.
                And he kept on taking too many aspirins.
                And he went on reading into all hours
                        of the morning.
He was a rebel
                and disrespectful
and
grandmother said he was going to end up all screwed up.
He sported a thick
                coffee-colored beard
                                peppered with grey.
He had a high forehead
                        a hooked nose
and soft white hair
that was always slicked back.

Just now I came across
that book
        on the shelf
LOST IN THE HIGH JUNGLES OF BORNEO
the pages are almost falling out
and the cover is missing.

No amaneció en su cama
y dejó la puerta de la cocina abierta.
Ese día me hicieron madrugar
y buscarlo por toda la casa
asomarme
                al brocal del pozo
                                y al hoyo del excusado
a registrar todo el patio.
Y forzado a oír los comentarios
de los grupos de vecinos que lamentaban la desaparición.
Y también al salir a la calle con el plato
a comprar los bollos de pan
                        contarle a mis amigos
                        que mi tío se había perdido
y que no iba a ir a clase
que llegaría a la escuela
                        sólo a pedirle permiso a la maestra
para buscar a mi tío que se había perdido.
Todos los muchachos se burlaban
y decían que mi tío no era chiquito para perderse.
Nuevamente veo los gorilas que roban mujeres.

It reminds me of when my uncle
got lost:
        He wasn't in his bed
and the kitchen door was left wide open.
That day they got me up early
to search the whole house for him.
I even peeked down
                the well
                      and down the shit-hole
and was looking all over the courtyard.
I had to listen to what all the neighbors were saying
as they gathered, very upset, over the disappearance.
Also I had to go down the street with a plate
to buy some rolls
              telling my friends
              that my uncle was lost
that I wasn't going to class
that I might just go to school
              to get the teacher's permission
to look for my lost uncle.
All the kids laughed at me
saying my uncle wasn't some little kid to get lost like that.

All over again
I see the gorillas who abduct women.

EL LIBRO DE LA HISTORIA DEL "CHE"

El libro de la historia del "CHE"
hijo de Augusto
hijo de Lautaro:
Lautaro
      "Inche Lautaro
      apubim ta pu huican"
      (Yo soy Lautaro que acabó con los españoles)
casado con Guaconda
y hermano a su vez de Caupolicán (El flechador del cielo)
y de Colocolo
engendró a Oropello;
Oropello engendra a Lecolón
y a sus hermanos;
Lecolón engendró a Cayeguano;
Cayeguano engendró a Talco;
Talco engendró a Rengo;
Rengo engendró a Túpac-Amaru;
Túpac-Amaru engendró a Túpac-Yupanqui
Túpac-Yupanqui engendró a Tucapel;
Tucapel engendró a Urraca de Panamá;
Urraca engendró a Diriangén de Nicaragua
y éste se suicidó
en las faldas del volcán Casitas
para nunca ser capturado
Diriangén engendró a Adiact
y éste fue colgado
en un palo de tamarindo que está en Subtiava
"Aquí murió el último jefe indio"
Y la gente de otras partes lo llega a ver como gran cosa
Adiact engendró a Xochitl Acatl (Flor de la caña)
Xochitl Acatl engendró a Guegue Miquistl (Perro Viejo)

THE BOOK OF "CHE"

The book of "Che"
son of Augusto
son of Lautaro:
Lautaro
                    "Inche Lautaro
                    apubim ta pu huican"
                    (I am Lautaro who finished off the Spaniards)
married to Guaconda
and brother, in turn, of Caupolicán (the celestial archer)
and of Colocolo,
Lautaro begat Oropello;
Oropello begat Lecolón
and his brothers;
Lecolón begat Cayeguano;
Cayeguano begat Talco;
Talco begat Rengo;
Rengo begat Túpac-Amaru;
Túpac-Amaru begat Túpac-Yupanqui;
Túpac-Yupanqui begat Tucapel;
Tucapel begat Urraca of Panama;
Urraca begat Diriangén of Nicaragua
and the latter committed suicide
on the slopes of the Casitas volcano
so he would never be captured.
Diriangén begat Adiact
and the latter was hanged
from a tamarind branch that is in Subtiaba.
"Here died the last Indian chief"
and folks from all over come to see it as a great thing
Adiact begat Xochitl Acatl (Cane Flower)
Xochitl Acatl begat Guegue Miquistl (Old Dog)

Guegue Miquistl engendró a Lempira;
Lempira engendró a Tecún-Umán;
Tecún-Umán engendró a Moctezuma Iluicámina;
Moctezuma Iluicámina engendró a Moctezuma Zocoyotlzin;
Moctezuma Zocoyotlzin engendró a Cuauhtémoc;
Cuauhtémoc engendró a Cuauhtemotzin
y éste fue ahorcado por los hombres de Cortés
y dijo:
> "Así he sabido
> lo que significa confiar
> en vuestras falsas promesas
> ¡oh Malinche! (Cortés)
> yo supe desde el momento
> en que no me di muerte
> por mi propia mano
> cuando entrásteis a mi ciudad
> de Tenochtitlán
> que me tenías reservado ese destino."

Cuauhtemotzin engendró a Quaupopoca;
Quaupopoca engendró a Tlacopán;
Tlacopán engendró a Huáscar;
Huáscar engendró a Jerónimo;
Jerónimo engendró a Pluma Gris;
Pluma Gris engendró a Caballo Loco;
Caballo Loco engendró a Toro Sentado;
Toro Sentado engendró a Bolívar;
Bolívar engendró a Sucre;
Sucre engendró a José de San Martín;
José de San Martín engendró a José Dolores Estrada;
José Dolores Estrada engendró a José Martí;
José Martí engendró a Joaquín Murrieta;

Guegue Miquistl begat Lempira;
Lempira begat Tecún-Umán;
Tecún-Umán begat Moctezuma Lluicámina;
Moctezuma Lluicámina begat Moctezuma Zocoyotlzin;
Moctezuma Zocoyotlzin begat Cuauhtémoc;
Cuauhtémoc begat Cuauhtemotzin
and the latter was hanged by Cortés' men
and he said:
> "So I learned
> what it means to believe
> your false promises
> oh Malinche! (Cortés)
> I knew from the moment
> I did not take my life
> with my own hand
> when you entered my city
> of Tenochtitlan
> that this was the fate
> you had in store for me."

Cuauhtemotzin begat Quaupopoca;
Quaupopoca begat Tlacopán;
Tlacopán begat Huáscar;
Huáscar begat Geronimo;
Geronimo begat Gray Feather;
Gray Feather begat Crazy Horse;
Crazy Horse begat Sitting Bull;
Sitting Bull begat Bolívar;
Bolívar begat Sucre;
Sucre begat José de San Martín;
José de San Martín begat José Dolores Estrada;
José Dolores Estrada begat José Martí;
José Martí begat Joaquín Murrieta;

Joaquín Murrieta engendró a Javier Mina;
Javier Mina engendró a Emiliano Zapata;
Emiliano Zapata engendró a Pancho Villa;
Pancho Villa engendró a Guerrero;
Guerrero engendró a Ortiz;
Ortiz engendró a Sandino;
Augusto César Sandino
hermano de Juan Gregorio Colindres
      y de Miguel Angel Ortez
      y de Juan Umanzor
      y de Francisco Estrada
      y de Sócrates Sandino
      y de Ramón Raudales
      y de Rufus Marín
y cuando hablaba decía:

      "Nuestra causa triunfará
      porque es la causa de la justicia
      porque es la causa del amor."
Y otras veces decía:

      "Yo me haré morir
      con los pocos que me acompañan
      porque es preferible
      hacernos morir como rebeldes
      y no vivir como esclavos."
Sandino engendró a Bayo;
el esposo de Adelita
del cual nació el "CHE"
que se llama Ernesto.

—1968/1969

Joaquín Murrieta begat Javier Mina;
Javier Mina begat Emiliano Zapata;
Emiliano Zapata begat Pancho Villa;
Pancho Villa begat Guerrero;
Guerrero begat Ortiz;
Ortiz begat Sandino;
Augusto César Sandino
brother of Juan Gregorio Colindres
        and of Miguel Angel Ortez
        and of Juan Umanzor
        and of Francisco Estrada
        and of Sócrates Sandino
        and of Ramón Raudales
        and of Rufus Marín
and when he spoke he said:
        "Our cause will triumph
        because it is the cause of justice
        because it is the cause of love."
and at other times he said:
        "I will die
        with the few who are with me
        we will die as rebels
        not live as slaves."
Sandino begat Bayo;
husband of Adelita
to whom was born "CHE"
who is called Ernesto.

        —1968/69

BIOGRAFÍA

Nunca apareció su nombre
en las tablas viejas del excusado escolar.
Al abandonar definitivamente el aula
nadie percibió su ausencia.
Las sirenas del mundo guardaron silencio,
jamás detectaron el incendio de su sangre.
El grado de sus llamas
se hacía cada vez más insoportable.
Hasta que abrazó con el ruido de sus pasos
la sombra de la montaña.
Aquella tierra virgen le amamantó con su misterio
cada brisa lavaba su ideal
y lo dejaba como niña blanca desnuda,
temblorosa, recién bañada.
Todo mundo careció de oídos y el combate
donde empezó a nacer
no se logró escuchar.

—1969

BIOGRAPHY

His name was never written
on the old walls of the school john.
When he left the classroom for good
nobody noticed he was gone.
The sirens of the world kept silent,
never detecting his blood on fire.
His fiery intensity
became more and more unbearable,
until the shadow of the mountains
embraced the sound of his footsteps.
That virgin land nurtured him with its mystery.
Each breeze cleansed his ideal
and left him like a child, naked and white
trembling, newly bathed.
The whole world was deaf, and where
the battle began to be born
no one listened.

—1969

LAS CASAS QUEDARON LLENAS DE HUMO

Ay patria
a los coroneles que orinan tus muros
tenemos que arrancarlos de raíces,
colgarlos en un árbol de rocío agudo,
violento de cóleras del pueblo.

—Otto René Castillo

A los héroes sandinistas:
  Julio Buitrago Urroz
  Alesio Blandón Juárez
  Marco Antonio Rivera Berríos
  Aníbal Castrillo Palma

Yo vi los huecos que la tanqueta Sherman
        abrió en la casa del barrio Frixione.
                Y despueés fui a ver más huecos
                en otra casa por Santo Domingo.
Y donde no había huecos de Sherman
        había huecos de Garand
                o de Madzen
                        o de Browning
o quién sabe de qué.
Las casas quedaron llenas de humo
        y después de dos horas
                Genie sin megáfono gritaba
                que se rindieran.
Y antes hacía como dos horas
y antes hacía como cuatro horas
y hacía como una hora
gritaba

THE HOUSES WERE STILL FULL OF SMOKE

Ay, my country,
the colonels who piss on your walls
we have to yank them out by the roots
hang them from a tree of bitter dew
violent with the rage of the people.

                                     —Otto René Castillo

To the Sandinista heroes:
   Julio Buitrago Urroz
   Alesio Blandón Juárez
   Marco Antonio Rivera Berríos
   Aníbal Castrillo Palma

I saw the holes the Sherman tank
       blew through the house in Frixione.
            And later I went to see more holes
            in another house near Santo Domingo.
And where there weren't holes from the Sherman
       there were holes from Garand rifles
          or from Madzens
                or Brownings
or from who knows what.
The houses were still full of smoke
       and after two hours
            General Genie, without a bullhorn, was shouting
            they should surrender.
And before, for about two hours
and before that, for about four hours
and for about an hour
he was shouting

                  y gritaba
                              y grita.
Que se rindieran.
Mientras la tanqueta
                  y las órdenes.
Las Browning
            las Madzen
                        las M-3
                                    los M-1
y las carretas
las granadas
                  las bombas lacrimógenas. . .
y los temblores de los guardias.

NUNCA CONTESTO NADIE
Porque los héroes nunca dijeron
                              que morían por la patria,
sino que murieron.

                                          —1969

                    shouting
                                and he's shouting
Surrender!
Meanwhile, the tank,
            its orders.
The Brownings
                the Madzens
                            the M-3's
                                        the M-1's
and the police wagons
the grenades
            the tear-gas cannisters. . .
and the Guardsmen shaking in their boots.

NOBODY EVER ANSWERED
Because the heroes never said
                        they would die for their country,
they just died.

                                —1969

RAMPAS Y RAMPAS Y RAMPAS

Ella
de la que tantas veces he abominado
¿Por qué no viene a satisfacer ahora
este deseo de morir purísimo que tengo?

—Ernesto Gutiérrez

Y casonas que casi juntan los aleros.
Haciendo cuevas de las calles.
Aceras altísimas
        y más arriba las puertas
                y sobre las puertas agujeros,
                      (flores, hojas, cuevas)
que tragan luz para las casas.
Desde el fondo de las casas
la bulla de los transistores
con las voces de alguna novela
                    o noticias
                        o canciones,
o tranquilos silencios
con los taburetes inmóviles
y las sillas playeras
                con sus espaldares secos,
y sus brazos untados de manteca con tierra
el asiento brillante también mantecoso.

El biombo repellado con pedazos de bolsas
Cemento Canal
partes de *La Prensa*
páginas de fotonovelas

RAMPS AND RAMPS AND RAMPS

Her,
the one who I've hated so many times,
why doesn't she come now to satisfy
this pure desire I have to die?

                              —Ernesto Gutiérrez

And large houses whose eaves almost meet.
Making caves of the streets.
High sidewalks
              higher doors
                         and above the doors, recesses
                                   (flowers, leaves, caves)
that swallow up light for the houses.
From deep within the houses
transistor radios blaring
with the voices of some soap-opera
                              or the news
                                        or songs,
or peaceful silences
among the heavy benches
and beach chairs
              with faded backs
their armrests smeared with grease and dirt
their shiny seats all greasy too.

The folding screen plastered with pieces of
Cemento Canal sacks
parts of *La Prensa*
pages from picture books

páginas de *Life*
carteles de cine.
La cortina en el centro meciéndose
                    para adentro y para afuera.
Raras veces dejando descubierto
el interior de las cuartos
con las cobijas colgadas
            y los zapatos viejos
                    y las bacinillas
                                embrocadas.

En la calle
el sol haciendo brillar el polvasal
            y la gente pasa con la espalda empapada.
Los zapatos lustrados se cubren
con una capa de polvo
y en el fondo
            un brillo.

En las esquinas eternas mangueras
apelmasando el polvo
            y la muchacha viendo donde cae el chorro
            y mojando las partes que aún quedan blanquiscas.

Rampas y rampas y rampas
y la línea férrea entre un polvasal.
Hacia el oeste el barrio va cambiando.
Hasta llegar a la iglesia del Calvario
                    y a una cancha de volibol
donde el sábado 21 de septiembre de 1956
Rigoberto López Pérez
                    jugó hasta las seis de la tarde
y cuando se fue

from *Life*
movie posters.
And the curtain in the middle blowing
                              in, out
now and then giving a glimpse
of the rooms inside
the hanging blankets
                    the old shoes
                              the chamber-pots
                                        turned upside down.

In the street
the swirling dust shines in the sun
                              folks pass by, their backs drenched.
Polished shoes coated
with a film of dust
with underneath
              a brilliance.

On the streetcorners eternal faucets
pack down the dust
              and the girl watching where the water falls
              soaking the spots where it's still bone dry.

Ramps and ramps and ramps
and train tracks in the swirling dust.
Towards the west the barrio keeps on changing
until it comes to Calvary Church
                              and a volleyball court
where on Saturday, September 21, 1956
Rigoberto López Pérez
              played until six in the evening
and when he left

limpiando la cara con un pañuelo
y las muchachas le hablaron
para que continuara jugando
él dijo:
"tengo que ir a hacer un volado."

—1969

               wiping his face with a handkerchief
and the girls tried to convince him
to keep on playing,
                he said:
"I have to go do something."

                            —1969

(Note: Rigoberto López Pérez, 21-year old Nicaraguan poet,
assassinated dictator Anastasio Somoza Debayle on Sept. 21, 1956,
and was killed immediately by the National Guard.)

LOS PANIQUINES ESTÁN VACÍOS

Los paniquines están vacíos
esperando alimentos. *Life*
les toma fotos a colores.
Los astronautas del Apolo 8
envían un mensaje de amor
desde la luna: "En la tierra paz
a los muertos de buena voluntad."

THE BASKETS ARE EMPTY

The baskets are empty
waiting for food. *Life*
takes color photos of them.
The astronauts of Apollo 8
send a message of love
from the moon: "Peace on earth
to the dead of good will."

DE IDA. . .

1.

Y desde arriba del puente
miraba al negro (en el lanchón
                            a orillas del muelle)
            que se tiraba al agua
y que salía con el calzoncillo blanco (blanquísimo)
                        pegado a la piel negra
            Que se tiraba al agua
y que salía
            (entre el montón de agua verde)
            con el calzoncillo blanco (blanquísimo)
                        pegado a la piel negra.
Y ahí estuvo
            tirándose
                    y tirándose
                            y tirándose
(desde el lanchón
            a orillas del muelle).
Yo me estuve
            viéndolo
                    y viéndolo
y me quedaba ido (casi dormido
desde arriba del puente
            del puente más largo de Nicaragua
            del puente sobre el río Siquia).
Y ahora me acuerdo que ese puente
                        tardó que lo hicieran
            y duró como cincuenta años para que lo terminaran
            o como cuarenta

THE JOURNEY OUT. . .

1.

And from up on the bridge
I was watching a black man (on the boat
                              at the side of the dock)
                    who threw himself into the water
and came out with white (white) underwear
                    stuck to his black skin.
                Who threw himself into the water
and came out
            (among the towering green waters)
            with white (white) underwear
                    stuck to his black skin
And there he was
                throwing himself
                    and throwing himself
                            throwing himself
(from the boat
            at the side of the dock).
And I was
        watching him
                and watching him
and I was gone (almost asleep
up on the bridge
                the longest bridge in Nicaragua
                bridge over the Siquia River).
And now I remember that that bridge
                            took so long being built
        it was something like fifty years before they finished it
        or maybe forty

o como veinte
o como que no me acuerdo cuántos
sólo me acuerdo que ese día (el día de la inauguración
                    de la inauguración del puente
                    del puente más largo de Nicaragua
                    del puente sobre el río Siquia)
toda *Novedades* salió llena de fotos
y en las fotos salía Somoza y el puente.
Pero en el cine se vio mejor
y se vio cuando él (el presidente) cortó la cinta
y dijo: "esto (4-) une el Pacífico con el Atlántico"
(4-) puente más largo de Nicaragua
            puente sobre el río Siquia.

2.

El lanchón dio vueltas
                y vueltas
                        y vueltas (sobre sí mismo)
sobre el río Siquia
cerca del puente más largo de Nicaragua
y por último no me di cuenta
si pasó por debajo del puente
o lo dejó atrás
al principio de las vueltas y vueltas del lanchón
estuve con la preocupación
y con la esperanza que al final de tanto vuelterío
pasara por debajo del puente
porque allí estaban unas muchachas lavando
y a una de las muchachas
le había visto las tetas de largo

or twenty
I don't remember how many
I just remember that one day (the day of the inauguration
                              the inauguration of the bridge
                              the longest bridge in Nicaragua
                              bridge over the Siquia River)
all the Somoza newspapers came out full of photos
and in the photos were Somoza and the bridge.
But in the movie newsreels you could see better
you saw when he (the President) cut the ribbon
and said: "This (Rte.4) unites the Pacific Coast
              with the Atlantic"
(Rte.4) the longest bridge in Nicaragua
              bridge over the Siquia River.

2.

The boat turned round
                    and turned
                              and turned round (on itself)
on the Siquia River
near the longest bridge in Nicaragua
until finally I didn't notice
if it had passed underneath the bridge
or had stayed behind
because when the boat began turning and turning
I was preoccupied
with the hope
that at the end of so much river-turning
it would pass under the bridge
because right there some girls were bathing
and I had seen the breasts of one of the girls
from far away

y se las había visto grandes
y se las quería ver de cerca.

3.

La rockonola pasó tronando todo el viaje
mientras el lanchón se deslizaba
como culebra (lento) sobre el río
y una negra piernuda
           con un negro
no pararon de hablar
           en voz baja
y en inglés
y sentados adelante
y riéndose a cada rato
           y hablando
           en voz baja
y en inglés.
Yo me paraba, me sentaba, caminaba
y me iba adelante
(de viaje adelante) por donde va el timón
para ver el río de frente
y allí miraba al negro recio que manejaba
y que no le interesaba el río
y que no le interesaba nada
y que parecía estatua
y que nunca supe para dónde miraba.

4.

Después de un gran oleaje en la bahía
donde el agua ya no era el agua bella del río
y que poco a poco el río se había ido ensanchando

and they looked big
and I wanted to see them up close.

3.

All during the journey rock'n'roll was blasting away
while the boat glided
like a snake (slow) on the river
and a bare-legged black girl
never stopped talking
               with a black man
               in a low voice
and in English
seated forward
laughing from time to time
               talking
               in a low voice
and in English.
I took it easy, sat down, walked around
I went forward
(for the forward journey) up to where the helm was
to see the river head-on
and there I saw the tough black guy who was steering
who wasn't interested in the river
who wasn't interested in anything
who seemed like a statue
and I never found out what he was looking toward.

4.

After a great rush of waves in the bay
where the water was no longer the beautiful water of the river
and little by little the river had been widening out

y perdiendo el color verde oscuro
                    verde oscuro y transparente
como pedazos de vidrio de las botellas de Cola "Shaler"
                    (verde oscuro y transparente)
y el olor a tierra suavemente humedecida
y los árboles
                    en las orillas tupidas de vegetación
y los árboles inclinados hasta el agua del río
como bebiendo agua
                    o como hindúes postrados ante el paso del Rajá
Y también perdiendo
                    su misterio de agua de río
que abriga culebras
                    y lagartos
su misterio fríío
                    y sus pozas heladas
con fondos confusos de árboles caídos
y ramerío
          y ramerío
y bejucales
y ramerío lamoso
                    y bejucales lamosos
y guindando grandes hilachas de lama
como pedazos de colchas viejas
zonas oscuras donde uno puede quedarse trabado
a varios cuerpos de profundidad.

Después de un gran oleaje en la bahía
donde el agua ya no era el agua bella del río
logramos llegar al muelle de Bluefields
allí donde grandes cantidades de basura flotan en el agua
y grandes cantidades de cerotes viejos

and losing its dark green color
        dark, transparent green
like pieces of glass from Shaler Cola bottles
        (dark, transparent green)
and the smell of the earth softly moistening
and the trees
        on the riverbanks dense with vegetation
the trees bending down towards the water of the river
as though they were drinking
        or were Hindus prostrate at the feet of their Raj
And losing also
        its river-water mystery
that shelters serpents
        and lizards
its cold mystery
        its icy pools
with their depths a tangle of fallen trees
and branches
        branches
and vines
muddy branches
        and muddy vines
and long gobs of slime hanging down
like squares of old quilts
dark areas
where you could stay bound
to all kinds of bodies in the deep.

After a great rush of waves in the bay
where the water was no longer the beautiful water of the river
we pulled into Bluefields, and docked:
there, where heaps of garbage float on the water
and heaps of old

                                        mojados
                                              carnosos
se mueven como bailando para acá y para allá
y para donde se mueve el agua
perseguidos por grandes cantidades de peje-sapo
perseguidos y picoteados
allí donde hay un muelle viejísimo
con las tablas todas quebradas
y en la primera bodega pegada al muelle
frente a la bahía
allí hay una gran foto
de Somoza sonriente
y no el viejo.

                    wet
                              pulpy turds
move as if dancing this way and that
and where the water moves pestered
by all the toad-slime
pestered and harassed
there, where there's a very old dock
with beat-up rotting planks
and on the first shack stuck to the dock
facing the bay
there's a big poster
of Somoza, smiling
and he's not the old man.

AGUANTANDO EL SOLAZO

tuve sed y me diste de beber
(frase célebre)

1.

Y cerros de cajillas de cerveza vacías
y cerros
        y cerros
y montones de cerros
            de cajillas de cervezas vacías
dando la impresión de cualquier desaparecida civilización india
dando la impresión de fabulosas pirámides
con largos sufrimientos de la intemperie
        las cajillas de cervezas vacías
            de pino
                blanquiscas
                nistes
                resecas
                tostadas
                rajadas por el sol
y sus bases tambíen blanquiscas
            llenas de gotitas de lodo
            zarpeadas de gotitas de lodo
                con gotitas
                        y gotitas
de lodo negrísimo.

UNDER THE SCORCHING SUN

"I was thirsty and you gave me drink."
                              (famous saying)

1.

And mounds of crates of empty beer bottles
and mounds
                and mounds
and mountains of mounds
                        of crates of empty beer bottles. . .
giving the impression of some lost Indian civilization
giving the impression of fabulous pyramids
long suffering from the elements
                        crates of empty beer bottles
                        pine crates
                                bleached
                                dried
                                parched
                                burnt
                                split by the sun
and their bottoms also bleached
                        full of splotches of mud
                        splattered with splotches of mud
                                with splotches
                                        and splotches
of black mud.

2.

Amarradas al muelle
      pangas
         o portátiles
         o motores
(como los caballos amarrados en las aceras de las ventas).
Y los pof-pof arrimando al muelle
                  lentamente
                  con sus bocanadas de humo
                  pof-pof-pof-pof-pof-pof-pof
                  con sus bocanadas de humo
                  lentamente
          arrimando al muelle.
Y un lanchón meciéndose suave
              y amarrado al muelle
y los negros zumbando cajillas de cervezas vacías
y otros acomodándolas en el lanchón
y el lanchón meciéndose suave
              y otros negros
              y negros
y más negros aventando
              y aventando
cajillas de cervezas llenas desde el lanchón
                  hasta el muelle
y en el muelle
      cerros
            y cerros
            y montones de cerros
de cajillas de cerveza llenas.
En el fondo
         en las tablas de las bodega
de la bodega que da al frente de la bahía
la gran risa de Somoza.

2.

Launches
       or sailboats
       or motorboats
tied to the dock
(like horses tied up at the hitching posts)
And the puff-puff pulling up to the dock
                        slowly
                        with its puffs of smoke
                        puff-puff-puff-puff-puff-puff
                        with its puffs of smoke
                        slowly
       pulling up to the dock.
And the boat rocking gently side to side
                  and tied to the dock
and black men heaving crates of empty beer bottles
and others stacking them up on the boat
and the boat rocking gently side to side
                  and other blacks
                  and blacks
and more black men lugging
              and lugging
crates of full beers from the boat
              down to the dock
and on the dock
        mounds
          and mounds
             mountains of mounds
of crates of full beers.
Behind it all
       on the walls of the store
of the store that faces the bay
Somoza's big smile.

79

3.

La primera cuadra toda llena de rótulos
comidería
      hospedaje
            Hong Kong
                  se vende
                        se compra
                              pulpería
Quan
    Morgan
        Chiong
           Chiang
               Campbell
                  Sujo
                    Hooker
                      Rigby.
La primera cuadra
        de subida
            y subida
y el sol dándole en la cara a uno
            y el sudor
            y el tufo
y el sol dándole en la cara a uno
                y el pavimento brillando con el sol
                    y derritiéndose con el sol
y el brillo dándole en los ojos
  el resplandor
  el calor insoportable
            y el sudor
y el tufo
y el sol dándole en la cara a uno
y uno

3.

The first block is packed with signs
Hong Kong
      food
           lodging
                 General Store
                         we buy
                              we sell
Quan
   Morgan
         Chiong
           Chiang
              Campbell
                   Sujo
                      Hooker
                         Rigby
The first block
         climbing uphill
            uphill
and the sun beating down on your face
               and the sweat
               the stink
and the sun beating down on your face
                  the sun reflecting off the pavement
                  the sweltering sun
and the reflection hitting you in the eyes
   the glare
   the unbearable heat
                 and the sweat
the stink
the sun beating down on your face
and you

                    pidiendo un poquito de agua
                              y el agua salobre.

4.

Después seguí caminando
aguantando el solazo
                    y el sudor
por las aceras
                    pero igual que caminar por en medio de las calles
porque las aceras parecen largas tiras de desierto
y ninguna acera tiene las sombras de los aleros
como aquí
                    y con el sol dándome en la cara
me di cuenta
                    que el estadio
                    el estadio de Bluefields se llama Somoza
y el sol arriba de la cuesta
y el sol dándome en la cara
y el sol dándome en los ojos
                    "sol sobre tapa sol pasando el tapa sol"
y a veces casi todo el día
                              una mosca zumbando bajo el sol
gente moviéndose como garrobos
                              solitarios bajo el sol
garrobos bajo el sol
                    gallos encendidos por el sol
                    paredes de adobe horneadas por el sol
                    yugos reventados por el sol
plumaje
        pelambre
                bramantes
                        piedras

           asking for a little water
                          and the water brackish.

4.

Later on, I continued walking
bearing up under the scorching sun
                          and the sweat
along the sidewalks
           but it's the same as walking in the middle of the street
because the sidewalks seem like long strips of desert
and there's no shade from the eaves
around here
                          and with the sun beating down on my face
I realized
                          that the stadium
                          the stadium in Bluefields is named Somoza
and the sun reflecting off the hill
and the sun beating down on my face
and the sun hitting me in my eyes
                          "sun times sun times sun times sun"
and almost all day long
                          a fly buzzing around under the sun
people moving around like lizards
                          solitary
                          under the sun
lizards under the sun
                          cocks inflamed by the sun
                          adobe walls baked by the sun
                          yokes broken by the sun
feathers
           hides
                      ropes
                              stones

quebrándose bajo el sol (Edwin Yllescas)
hasta que llegué a un parque
donde está un tornapool viejo
y una estatua de Rigoberto Cabezas
                    o de Zelaya
o quien sabe de quién.

splitting apart under the sun (Edwin Yllescas)
until I came to a park
where there's an old fountain
and a statue of Rigoberto Cabezas
                              or of Zelaya
or someone or other.

PARA QUE SE DEN CUENTA

—Sí pero no tocamos
—No se ve cuando se toca, dijimos.
        Vamos,
sigamos viendo cuanto vimos.

—Carlos Martínez Rivas

Hace bastante vi las piernas de una muchacha.
Como los dientes de leche eran blanquísimas,
semejantes no sé en qué al vidrio pulido
de un carro nuevo.

                Me quedé ido
hasta que ella hizo el vano intento
de alargarse el vestido.

Yo continué explicando:
"para aprender matemáticas es necesario
absoluta concentración." Comencé a demostrar
el Teorema del Residuo, o el de Pitágoras
o el de Ruffini.

No resistí continuar
y al rato consideraba lo fresco, lo húmedo,
lo suave de las piernas de aquella muchacha.

Cuando me callaba, todos pensaban
que resolvía una abstracción matemática.
Pero yo veía las piernas,
casi todos los días le veía las piernas,
y nunca pude tocárselas.

—1969

SO YOU'LL KNOW

"Yes, but don't touch."
"You can't see when you touch," we said.
"Come on,
let's keep looking, we saw so much."
—Carlos Martínez Rivas

A while ago I saw the legs of a girl.
Like baby teeth they were pure white
resembling—I don't know—the polished windows
of a new car.

I was dazed
until she made a vain attempt
to pull her skirt down.

I went on explaining:
"to grasp mathematics absolute concentration
is necessary." I began to demonstrate
the Remainder Theorum, or the Pythagorean Theorum,
or Ruffini's.

I didn't stop talking
and, from time to time, I thought about the fresh, moist
softness of that girl's legs.

When I did stop, they all thought
I had solved some mathematical abstraction.
But I was looking at her legs,
just about every day I looked at her legs
and I never could touch them.

—1969

COMO LOS SANTOS

Ahora quiero hablar con ustedes
o mejor dicho
ahora estoy hablando con ustedes.

Con vos
con vos tunco carretonero
con vos estoy hablando.

Con vos carbonero
              carbonero encontilado
     vos
     vos que llevás ese cipote
                        enganchado
                        sobre el carretón
y lo llevás sosteniendo la lata
y todo encontilado.

Vos amarraste una vez
              hace tiempo
              un trapo
              un trapo acabado de lavar
              todo ajado
              ajado y niste
y que lo amarraste en uno de los brazos del carretón
              para secarte el sudor
                   y la tierra
                   y el tilde
                   y todo revuelto
y el trapo
está mugroso

LIKE THE SAINTS

Now I want to talk with you
or rather
now I am talking with you

With you
with you, pork peddler
I'm talking with you

With you, charcoal seller
            charcoal seller covered in soot
      you
      you who carry that youngster
                                    hitched
                                    on top of your cart
and you cart it enduring the boredom
and everything all sooty

One time
            a while ago
            you tied up a rag
            a rag that had just been washed
            all wrinkled
            wrinkled and stained
you tied it to one of the poles of the cart
            to wipe away your sweat
            the dirt
            the censure
            the whole mess
and the rag
is filthy

y hasta echa un olor a agrio
que vos lo sentís de viaje
                    cuando te secas la cara
                    o el pescuezo.
A vos te hablo
a vos que te suben el rango de la miseria
cada vez que te sale otra tira guindando del pantalón
vos que sos marca mundial
en el récord de los ayunos
¡qué cuarenta días!
¡y qué cuarenta noches!
A vos que se te asoma
curioso el calzoncillo nacido
                    por todo lo roto del pantalón
y hay gente que sale a la puerta
                    y que se pone a reír
hasta que doblás la esquina
chapaleando tufo
y seguís empujando
y con las rodillas peladas
y con el pecho consumido
                    y desnudo.
Con vos estoy hablando
con vos mismo
sí, sí
        a vos te digo.

Con vos también
            aseado chofer particular
            engrasado taxista
            camionero polvoso
            busero gordo
            soldador borracho

and gives off a bitter stink
that you smell as you go
      when you wipe your face
               or your neck
I'm speaking to you
to you who come up through the ranks of misery
each time with more shreds hanging from your pants
you who hold the world's record
in the record book of fasting:
what a forty days!
and what a forty nights!
To you whose underwear comes
clean through
      the complete defeat of your pants
and people come to their doorways
      who start to laugh
as you turn the corner
splattering foul smelling
and you keep on pushing
      with your knees bare
      your naked, tubercular chest
I'm speaking with you
you yourself
yes, yes
with you
     I'm speaking

With you too
      clean private chauffeur
      greasy taxidriver
      dusty truckdriver
      fat busdriver
      drunken welder

zapatero remendón
judío errante afilador de cuchillos
                               de hachas
                               machetes y tijeras
con todos los vende sorbetes y raspados
y con todos los vendedores ambulantes.

Con vos también
                 cipote vende chicles
                 y con el otro
                 el que vende bolis congelados
                 y el que vende gelatinas
                 y también con el de la bolsa de confites de coco
y con el de la bolsa de leche de burras
y con todos los lustradores vulgares
(aunque digan que más vulgar es mi madre)
y también háblenle a los ciegos
                 a los ciegos que piden limosna en las paradas
                 y a los otros ciegos de guitarras o sin guitarras
                 (y a los proletarios de la música)
                 y a los tullidos de toda clase
                 y a los tísicos del estadio
                 y a los mudos y sordos de nacimiento.

Pásenle la voz a los basucas
y díganles que vengan
llamen a los chivos sifilíticos
y a los rateros
y a los busca pleitos en las cantinas
en los estancos y en los putales
tráiganse también
a toda la mancha de vagos
a todos los vagos de todos los barrios

shoemaker
wandering jew sharpener of knives
hatchets
machetes and scissors
with everyone who sells sherbets and ices
and with all the street peddlers

With you too
kid selling chiclets
and with the other one
the one selling frozen snowcones
and the one selling gumdrops
and also the one with his bag of coconut sweets
and the one with a bag of caramels
and with all the common shoeshine boys
(though they say my mother's even more common)
And also, let's talk to those who are blind
to the blind who beg for alms at bus stops
and to the others also blind, with guitars or without
(to the proletarians of music)
and to the crippled of every kind
and to the tubercular wards of the State
and to those deaf and dumb from birth

Let the garbage collectors know
and speak to them who come
call out the syphilitic kids
and the petty thieves
the troublemakers in the bars
in the smokeshops and whorehouses
and bring with you also
the whole motley crew of do-nothings
all those hanging around in all the barrios

que ahorita están jugando janbol
y si no desmoche
aunque se quede el que tenga mico doble
que se vengan todos los demás
y aunque estén esperando con dos embolones.

Que se vengan todos los que están bateando
y los que están sirviendo
que se deshagan las apuestas
y que vengan
y que bajen las pandillas de todos lados.

SAQUEN A TODOS LOS ESQUELETOS

a todos los esqueletos que se mueran
en Los Cauces
en Miralagos
en el Valle Maldito
en Acahualinca
en La Fortaleza
en El Fanguito
en las Calles del Pecado
en La Zona
en La Perla
en la colonia Alta Vista
en la colonia López Mateos
en La Salinera
en Cabo Haitiano
en La Fossette
y que traigan a sus cipotes
a sus cipotes que "no nacen por hambre
y que tienen hambre de nacer
para morirse de hambre"

                    who right now are playing handball
                    and if the game can't be cut short
though the one who has both sides covered stays
all the rest should come
though you're only two points away from winning

Come on, everyone who's hitting
                    and those who are serving
drop your bets
                    and come on
and the gangs should come on down from all over

BRING OUT ALL THE SKELETONS

all the skeletons who die
                    in Los Cauces
                    in Miralagos
                    in Valle Maldito
                    in Acahualinca
                    in La Fortaleza
                    in El Fanguito
                    in Calles del Pecado
                    in La Zona
                    in La Perla
                    in Alta Vista
                    in López Mateos
                    in La Salinera
                    in Cabo Haitiano
                    in La Fossette
and bring out your kids
your kids who "because of hunger aren't born
                    but who hunger to be born
                    only to die of hunger"

Que vengan todas las mujeres
      la verdulera nalgona
      y la vieja asmática del canasto
      la negra vende vigorón
      y la sombreruda vende baho
      la vende chicha helada
      y la vende cebada
      la vende naranjada
      y la lavandera con las manos blanquiscas de jabón
      las poncheras de la fiesta
      y las vende gallo pinto y carne asada
      las mondongueras
      y las nacatamaleras mantecosas
      las sirvientas
      las picheles
      las rufianas
      con todo y sus zorras
y aquella muchacha hermosa que vende pan con mantequilla
y la chavalita
         que está empezando a echar tetitas
         y que vende pasteles
y todas las cipotas que venden guineos
               naranjas
               y mandarinas
               y que por un peso dan una bolsa.
Que vengan también las carteristas
      las cantineras
      y las putas
      y las putas viejas y tetonas
      y las putas iniciadas
háblenle a las espiritistas
      y a las medium
      y a las endemoniadas

All the women should come
       the fat-assed fishwife
       and the asthmatic old woman with the baskets
       the black woman selling cold drinks
       and the woman in the shade selling trinkets
       the seller of cold *chicha*
       and the seller of bait
       the woman selling orangeade
       and the laundress with her hands bleached from soap
       the barmaids at parties
       and the sellers of rice and beans and barbecue
       the ones selling dried tripe
       and the makers of greasy tamales
       the servants
       the waitresses
       the madames
       all of them and their foxes
and that beautiful girl there who's selling bread and butter
and the little kid
       who's beginning to develop breasts
       who sells pastries
and all the kids who sell bananas
              oranges
              tangerines
              and give for a penny a paper bag
All the pickpockets should come
       the 'B-girls'
       and the whores
       the old whores with big tits
       and the whores just starting out
Let's talk to the spiritualists
       and to the mediums
       the women possessed by demons

a las perseguidas por los duendes
y por los malos espíritus
a las hechiceras
y a las hechizadas
a las vende filtros
y a las compra filtros.
Ahora que están todos aquí
que están todos aquí reunidos
reunidos y oyéndome,
ahora quiero hablar con ustedes
o mejor dicho
ahora estoy hablando con ustedes
quiero empezar a hacerles una plática
y quiero que todos ustedes
le platiquen
a todos los que no vinieron
y que les platiquen en voz alta cuando estén solos,
y que les platiquen en las calles
en las casas
en los buses
en los cines
en los parques
en las iglesias
en los billares
en los patios montosos
en los barrios sin luz
y a orilla de los cercos que se están
cayendo
y a orilla de los ríos
sentados en las cunetas
arrimados en las mochetas de las puertas
y asomados por las ventanas

and those persecuted by goblins
and by evil spirits
and to the witches
to the bewitched
to those who sell love-potions
and those who buy them
Now that you are all here
all gathered here together
together and listening to me
now I want to speak with you
or rather
now I am speaking with you
I want to begin a discussion with you
and I want you too
to discuss it
with everyone who didn't come
and discuss it loudly when you're alone
and discuss it in the streets
the houses
the buses
the movies
the parks
churches
pool halls
crowded courtyards
barrios with no lights
and along the walls that are crumbling
on the banks of the rivers
sitting in ditches
hunkered down in doorways
and leaning out windows

y en fin
   en todas partes
y que platiquen en voz baja
                    cuando no estén solos
o mejor dicho cuando está un rico cerca
o cuando está un guardia de un rico cerca.

Yo les quería platicar
que ahora vivo en las catacumbas
y que estoy decidido a matar el hambre que nos mata
cuando platiquen esto
platíquenlo duro
cuando no esté uno de los que siembra el hambre
o un oreja de los que siembra el hambre
o un guardia de los que siembra el hambre.

Cállense todos
y síganme oyendo
              en las catacumbas
              ya en la tarde cuando hay poco trabajo
              pinto en las paredes
              en las paredes de las catacumbas
              las imágenes de los santos
              de los santos que han muerto matando el hambre
              y en la mañana imito a los santos.
Ahora quiero hablarles de los santos.

SANDINO

"Había un nica de Niquinohomo
que no era ni político
                    ni soldado"

and finally
            everywhere
and discuss it in a low voice
                when you are not alone
or rather
when there's a rich man nearby
or when there's a rich man's guard nearby

I would like to discuss with you
how now I live in the catacombs
and how determined I am to kill the hunger that is killing us
when you discuss this
discuss it long and hard
when no one who sows hunger is around
nor a spy for those who sow hunger
nor a guard for those who sow hunger

Quiet, all of you
and follow me listening
                in the catacombs
                now, in the afternoons, when there's not much work
                I paint on the walls
                the walls of the catacombs
                images of the saints
                the saints who died killing hunger
                and in the morning I imitate the saints
Now I want to talk to you about the saints:

SANDINO

"There was a Nica from Niquinohomo
who was neither a politician
                        nor a soldier"

luchó en Las Segovias
y una vez que le escribió a Froylán Turcios
le decía que si los yanquis
por ironía del destino
le mataban a todos sus guerrilleros
en el corazón de ellos
encontraría el tesoro más grande de patriotismo
y que eso humillaría a la gallina
que en forma de águila
ostenta el escudo de los norteamericanos
y más adelante le decía
que por su parte al verse solo (cosa que no creía)
se pondría en el centro de cien quintales de dinamita
que tenía en su botín de guerra
y que con su propia mano daría fuego
y que dijeran a cuatrocientos kilómetros a la redonda:

SANDINO HA MUERTO.

EL "CHE"

"Ni un tanque
ni una bomba de hidrógeno
ni todas las bolitas del mundo"
lucha en todas partes
y en todas partes
florecen las higueras
del río bajan montones de guerrilleros
en Higueras del Río dicen que lo mataron
"CHE" comandante
nosotros somos el camino
y vos el caminante.

He fought in Las Segovias
and one time when he wrote to Froylán Turcios
he told him that if the Yankees
by some irony of fate
killed all his guerrillas,
they would find in their hearts
the great treasure of patriotism
and that it would humiliate the chicken
who shows off like an eagle
on the North American coat of arms.
And further he said
that for his part if he found himself alone
(something he didn't believe)
he would put himself in the middle of a hundred sticks of dynamite
that he kept in his war-chest
and with his own hand he would ignite it
so that for four hundred kilometers around they would say:
SANDINO HAS DIED.

CHE

"Not a tank
not a hydrogen bomb
nor all the ballots in the world"
He fights everywhere
and everywhere
the *higueras* bloom
mountains of guerrillas descend on the river
in *Higueras del Río* they say they killed him
CHE, commander,
we are the path
and you the one who walks it.

MIGUEL ANGEL ORTEZ

"Y aún hecho ya polvo
se miaban de pánico los yanquis"
al comienzo Sandino no lo quería aceptar
pero él le dijo a Sandino
que él era el capitán Ferrerita
y después del combate de Ocotal
le dio una mula blanca
y se le pegó
hasta que llegó a ser
el general del coro de ángeles
murió en Palacagüina peleando mano a mano.

JORGE NAVARRO

Fue tan valiente como para no morir de tristeza.
Hablaba en las asambleas
y una vez hizo un periódico
tenía un acordeón
pero sabía que hay un deber de cantar
y otro de morir
murió con los pies engusanados
por el lodo de Bocaycito
pero resucitó
el mismo día
y por todas los lados.

MIGUEL ANGEL ORTEZ

"And even when he was already dust
the Yankees mewed like kittens in panic"
At first Sandino didn't want him
but he told Sandino
he was Captain Ferrerita
and after the fighting in Ocotal
Sandino gave him a white mule
and he drove it
until he came to be
General of the Choir of Angels
He died in Palacagüinia, fighting hand to hand.

JORGE NAVARRO

He was so brave, so as not to die of sorrow.
He used to speak at meetings
and at one time he put out a newspaper
he had an accordion
because he knew one had a duty to sing
as well as to die
he died with his feet covered with worms
in the mud of Bocaycito
but that same day
he was resurrected
everywhere.

SELIM SHIBLE

Conociste a Selim.
Sabías que una vez verguió a un agente de la seguridad
en la propia oficina de seguridad
si no sabías eso
no conociste a Selim
cuando llegó a vivir por nosotros
¡murió en la perfecta manera que nació!
pero ya desde 'antes
desde hacía siglos era eterno.

JACINTO BACA

Con el brazo izquierdo de mampuesta
y con el derecho disparando su pistola
sí señores
hay una patrulla de JACINTOS arpillando al enemigo
y una gran estatua
aunque rota ya su sangre
creció en una plaza de Rota.

JULIO BUITRAGO

Nunca contestó nadie
porque los héroes no dijeron
que morían por la patria
sino que murieron
en julio nació Julio
seis más nueve quince
de seis y nueve sesenta y nueve

SELIM SHIBLE

You knew Selim.
Did you know that one time he beat up a security agent
inside his own security office?
If you didn't know that
you didn't know Selim.
When he came to live through us
he died in the perfect way he was born!
But now, as for centuries before
he is eternal.

JACINTO BACA

With his left arm taking aim
and his right firing the pistol
yes gentlemen
there's a band of JACINTOS sacking the enemy
and (even though it's shattered now)
a big statue
that rose from his blood in the Plaza de Rota.

JULIO BUITRAGO

No one ever answered
because the heroes never said
they would die for their country
they just died.
Julio was born in July
six and nine make fifteen
on the six and nine of sixty-nine

nació matando al hambre (aunque sea antipoético)
nació peleando solo
contra trescientos
es el único que nació en el mundo
superando a Leónidas
a Leónidas el de las Termópilas

"VIAJERO VE Y DI A ESPARTA A QUE MORIMOS
POR CUMPLIR SUS SAGRADAS LEYES."

ESO ESTA EN LA CASA
DONDE NACIO JULIO
lo único que está en español
pues sí
nació sin camisa
        y cantando mientras disparaba su M-3
     nació cuando trataban de matarlo
           con guardias
           con tanques
           con aviones
     nació cuando no pudieron matarlo
        y esto cuéntenselo a todo el mundo
y esto cuéntenselo a todo el mundo
platíquenlo duro
platíquenlo duro siempre
duro siempre
con la tranca en la mano
con el machete en la mano
con la escopeta en la mano.
¡Ya platicamos!

AHORA VAMOS A VIVIR COMO LOS SANTOS.

—1969

he was born killing hunger
(though it's anti-poetic)
he was born fighting alone
against three hundred
he was the only one born in the world
surpassing Leonidas
Leonidas of Thermopylae.

"TRAVELER GO AND TELL SPARTA
WE DIE FULFILLING HER SACRED LAWS"

THAT WAS IN THE HOUSE
WHERE JULIO WAS BORN
only it was in Spanish
and yes
he was born without a shirt
                and was singing while he fired his M-3
        he was born when they tried to kill him
                                with the Guard
                                with tanks
                                with planes
        he was born when they were not able to kill him
                this story you should tell to everyone
you should tell this story to everyone
you should discuss it long and hard
you should discuss it hard forever
forever hard
with a stick in your hand
with a machete in your hand
with a shotgun in your hand
let's discuss it now!

NOW LET US LIVE LIKE THE SAINTS

                                        —1969

EPITAFIO

Aquí yacen
los restos mortales
del que en vida
buscó sin alivio
una
a
una
tu cara
en todos
los buses urbanos.

noviembre/diciembre de 1969

EPITAPH

Here lie
the mortal remains
of one who in life
searched without relief for
one
by
one
your face
on every
bus in the city.

november/december 1969

Nicaraguan women and a poem by Rugama.

photograph: Margaret Randall

AFTERWORD

Doña Candida Rugama, mother of Leonel Rugama, was interviewed in 1983 by Juan José Godoy, a North American writer, living in Estelí, Nicaragua. In the following excerpts, Candida Rugama talks about her son.

From the time he was a little boy, he was sharp, ready to answer whatever you asked him about. . .he'd have conversations with you like an adult. He was witty. A joker, as he would say. And he loved to go to the circus. He always wanted to watch the circus people working, setting up the tents, getting the animals ready. He hung around talking with them, asking them a million questions. . .

He had wanted to study civil engineering. When he finished primary school, he wanted to take math classes so he could enter the seminary. I tried to talk him out of it, because we had so little money: but he was determined and I gave in. With the few pennies we had coming in from a small pension, he'd buy books and put them in his bookbag—he loved classes, and he had a regular ritual about going to school. First he would bathe, then he'd go and study some more—he had every minute of his day planned out for what he had to do.

He passed the pre-seminary courses in San Ramón High School in León, where he met Omar Cabezas. Later, it seemed he didn't want to study. He. . .who knows what difficulties he saw there. And he told me that he was going to get this diploma here, which he did, in the Francisco Luis Espinoza High School. He graduated as the best student in his class. He began to study German, and thought about getting a scholarship so he could go study in Germany. But already he had his ideals: because according to Father Cardenal, who was in the seminary, Leonel used to visit the poorest barrios in Managua. It was seeing the poverty there, said Father Cardenal, that gave birth to Leonel's ideas of service: that was where his love for humanity came from. And from that time on he demonstrated his caring. With the kids who couldn't pay for math lessons with him, he'd give them free lessons and lend them his own books. With students poorer than he was, he wound up giving them his clothes.

But the scholarship didn't come through. When he had already been accepted, someone went to the school and denounced Leonel as a leftist, and they wouldn't give him the scholarship. So he decided to enter the University in León, but not to get a degree the way he wrote and told his father, but to work for the revolution. . .he enrolled in the University under the name of "Francisco" instead of Leonel: he said he was Leonel Rugama's brother, and that's how he was able to get in.

He became a member of the FER: the student group that did revolutionary work in the high schools and in the University. Later on, he entered the FSLN. . .They tell me that when he was in the University he used to walk around with his Bible under his arm and a stack of newspapers—so if he got caught at night, he could sleep under the papers. And people would give him, say, five *córdobas* for his FER expenses, and he'd eat with two and use the rest to buy ammunition. When a friend told Leonel that there was going to be a party and the tickets were ten *córdobas*, he answered, "No! with ten *córdobas* I can buy a box of bullets."

The entire year he was at the University he hadn't been back to Estelí. By 1970 he was in Managua with three other comrades preparing to go to the mountains with the guerrillas. They had collected provisions and plenty of weapons.

He was with Mauricio Hernández Baldizón, Roberto Núñez Dávila, and Igor Ubeda, a boy from our town. And they found out that someone had turned them in to the Guard.

The daughter of a woman whose son was also a Sandinista went to warn them, bringing them food. When she saw them she shouted, "Muchachos, here comes the Guard!" They grabbed their guns—Igor Ubeda made it out and escaped to Estelí.

The Guard surrounded the house. There were about three hundred soldiers, for the three of them left in the house. The fighting lasted from one in the afternoon until about five, with tanks and bombs and helicopters. The Chief of Security kept calling to them with a bullhorn, ordering them to surrender. Finally, Leonel answered: "Tell your mother to surrender!"

They say that was his finest poem. His last verse. A little later people heard them singing the Sandinista hymn.

The other two were killed first. Leonel was dying when one of the guardsmen came in through a hole the tanks had blasted open in the side of the house, and finished him off with a bullet. He died on January 15, 1970, before making it to his twenty-first birthday.

AFTERWORD

Comandante Omar Cabezas, a Sandinista guerrilla leader and the author of Nicaragua's popular classic *La Montaña es Algo Más que una Inmensa Estapa Verde* (which is now available in English, translated by Kathleen Weaver and published by Crown Publishers under the title *Fire from the Mountain*), has written about his relationship with Leonel Rugama in that book. The following excerpts are interwoven with an interview with Cabezas by Margaret Randall, poet, author, photographer.

. . .I knew Leonel Rugama, but I didn't remember him until I really got to know him through my buddy, Manuel Noguera, a good friend of mine who was a great judge of character. Manuel walked by one day during Easter Week while we were sitting on the grass in León's central park, eating ices.

Leonel and I needed to talk, but not in a public place like Prio's, because I was already going to demonstrations and my father was an outspoken opposition figure, and we couldn't talk at Lezama's and we didn't want to walk around the streets in the scorching sun. So we had to go to the park, find a shady tree and sit on the grass because it was the coolest place in the whole city for a poor person, since there were hardly any trees in León and we certainly didn't have air-conditioning in my house, only the University was air-conditioned and it was closed because not even Victor, the janitor, stayed there during Easter Week.

Do you follow me? We were talking things over in the park because it was Easter Week in León.

And standing there was Manuel, and he directed his greeting towards my companero: "Hey! Leonel! And Omar was trying to tell me your name was Marcial Ocampo!"

"Who's Leonel?" he answered. "My name is Marcial."

"You can't fool me! You're Leonel Rugama! Don't you remember we studied together in San Ramón?"

"Holy shit," I said, "Leonel Rugama, no kidding. I remember you. You owe me twenty pesos worth of bread."

. . .At the University I had an imaginary dog. I was always playing around with it, with my hand out, see, like this. . . "This here dog. . ." "What dog?" "This one! Don't you have any sense of humor?" I'd say. Leonel in the beginning resented the whole thing about my dog. Then, later on, they all became fond of it: they borrowed the dog, they even brought it home. It was a group craziness I invented. One time I loaned Leonel something and was bugging him to return it. So he says to me, "That son-of- a-bitch dog of yours chewed it to bits."

. . .Leonel's way of horsing around was a style we had, a way of talking, a way of having fun, a way of acting. Each of us, with his particular personality, left his mark on the group. Leonel had a way of living. . .He was like Roque Dalton: as far as I know, he hadn't been a friend of Roque's; they didn't know each other. I used to think Roque was influenced by Leonel, but it must have been the other way around. Anyway, the way Leonel and Roque wrote had an enormous influence on me.

As Leonel matured, he always aimed for the one sole thing that became the most important aspect of his personality. Leonel dealt with the matter of being a man: not a macho-man, but a man who bears a sense of historical responsibility. A man who's committed to others, who gives everything for the happiness of others. Leonel's guiding star was Ernesto Ché Guevara, who'd just been killed. He laid out for me the basis of all his political thought: the duty we have to free man from the poverty, the exploitation, from the rising death toll of revolutionaries— he laid it all out for me.

I remember the day there was an ideological debate at the University, and I approached one of the small groups Leonel had formed where he was leading a heated discussion. Leonel was a Marxist-Leninist by then, and an anticleric. I remember how he knitted his brows, frowning, and argued with the others, "You have to be like Ché. . .be like Ché. . .be like Ché. . .be like Ché. . ." His gestures, his features, his words were explosives, loaded with the feeling he carried around inside him, and they had an impact on me. It hit the very center of my brain: "be like Ché. . .be like Ché. . ." I left the University with that phrase repeating itself in my head as if it was a tape recording, remembering so clearly Leonel's gestures, his facial expressions, and the firmness as he declared, "You have to be like Ché."

. . .Leonel Rugama left his mark on certain aspects of my conduct. He added nuances to my personality. I was influenced by Leonel, but not just in a literary way: in my life. Something more universal than literature. I was influenced by Leonel's personality, by a life style, a way of thinking, of making things happen: a way of encountering the *feeling* of things.

. . .I began to write, but I didn't know how. I never really read literature, I never had the patience. . .It has to do with Leonel. Because we had fun with a whole world of things, and years later I'd be thinking how he would have liked this and that. And I thought "All this shit is going to be lost: and the epic of the mountains, and our struggle. . ." I always thought of literature in connection with Leonel—he read all the "boom" writers, and he also yelled at us for not reading Marxism. . . So I began to write: for Leonel. The whole thing has something to do with him.

THE STUDENT AND REVOLUTION

Revolution

The broad concept of revolution implies the change of pre-established norms: norms that pertain to an individual, to a group of individuals or to many groups as a whole.

Every revolution can be regarded as a function of human evolution, inasmuch as the evolutionary process goes along at an astounding velocity, and the vehicle that holds man becomes an obstacle to his own evolution: he must smash it, just as he must smash the forgers of its limit.

The trajectory from the expansion of the idea up to the moment of change is what revolution is.

If there are norms which obstruct or pervert full or partial human development, the revolution must be set in motion to achieve, for the most part, human integrity.

This revolution includes (and engages) all those affected by existing norms: it is our duty to defend ourselves. To not set the revolution in motion against crushing, destructive norms is suicidal, given that the revolution has the capability to destroy norms that are killing us.

The revolution also engages visionaries who are not directly affected by the harshness of the norms. But if they are aware of that harsh reality, they must launch the revolution. Otherwise the oppressed simply die, ignorant of the real reasons for their death, and the blame falls then on the visionaries, who become criminals.

Types of Revolution

Throughout history revolution has taken two forms:

a) Peaceful revolutions, that is, those which pursue a change without the use of physical force and with a strained, intense intellectual force. A classic example of this is Ghandi's revolution in India; Christianity, also, established itself on the basis of a peaceful revolution.

Pacifism does not suppose a lack of combativeness in revolutionary struggle; on the contrary, often the reprisals and obstacles it encounters are enormous.

b) Violent revolutions: they are the product of a maximum state of oppression, when a violent revolution becomes the only path men have left to take. If, with the triumph of violent revolution, we have not fully realized ourselves, at least we have acted so our children may fully realize themselves and their human dignity.

In violent revolution, the power of physical force rules. But it is absolutely necessary that it be controlled directly by the intellect. The revolution triumphs only when brute force is combined with intellectual work.

Fields of the Revolution

The fields in which the revolution develops are many and diverse.

The most compact field of a revolution is the subjective field, but just because it is compact doesn't mean it poses fewer difficulties: there are bloody struggles waged on behalf of the triumph of an inner revolution.

Later on the revolution turns up in marriage, in the home, in the district or barrio, in the county or city, in the nation, on the continent and throughout the universe.

All these revolutions conform to one single revolution. Nevertheless, for someone liberated in his inner self, the personal revolution can be called the *first revolution*.

Generally, one ascends the revolution by degrees, achieving an effective triumph at each step of the way. With the success of the personal revolution the individual acquires a rational vision of events. These, naturally, come to be seen as either desirable or undesirable. Every field is full of sacrifices and pitfalls, and it is only possible to go forward hardening the will—sanctifying force of the revolutionary. The harshness of struggle alone, from the ground up, is what allows us to feel revolution.

Stages of the Revolution

Every revolution goes through two fundamental stages. The greater the revolution, the greater the hardship will be. The larger the change posed by the revolution, the more rigorous its stages will be. Essentially, I believe there are two very distinctive stages through which every revolution must pass:

a) Destruction, and b) Construction.

a) *Destruction*. When one pursues a change, it is necessary to clear a site on which to do it. This clearing is called destruction. The greater the change, the more terrain that will have to be cleared. But no matter how small the change may be, the destructive stage has always a hint of suffering.

b) *Construction*. Once the first stage is finished, the cleared terrain is ready for change. During the constructive stage we have to anticipate and win over two power-groups that attempt to impede revolutionary progress. The first group is made up of those people who want to reconstruct exactly what has been already destroyed, people who refuse to conform, and who only want to satisfy their own personal needs and luxuries. The second groups is comprised of opportunists who, seeing the terrain cleared, attempt to usurp it for their own well-being.

The transcendence of this stage becomes most evident with a simple affirmation: to construct requires more intuition and skill than to destroy.

Classes of Revolution

Revolutions fall into two classes. The first class comes about when changes are absolutely necessary and inevitable, and when one proposes substituting human norms with totally humanizing laws. This revolution is set in motion by honest individuals who don't want to commit suicide by following familiar norms. Also those so-called visionaries—people who refuse to stain their hands with the indelible blood of the oppressed—play an active role in this revolution.

The second class of revolution comes about when changes are unnecessary and counter-productive. It seeks to replace necessary norms with bestial-destructive laws. This revolution is brought about by oppressors who seek their own petty and transitory well-being. Generally, it is carried out by mercenaries and criminals for profit.

Steadfast Revolutionaries

Revolutions have had, have, and will have individuals who are steadfast. In just revolutions, there are people with a noble, revolutionary calling and with a spirit of sacrifice in accord with a strong will. As I see it, a revolutionary with such a nature is a militant saint on the side of humanity.

"This type of struggle gives us the opportunity to turn ourselves into revolutionaries, the highest level of the human species, but it also allows us to live as men."—Ernesto Guevara

"As if the struggle isn't the noblest of songs and death the greatest."—Fernando Gordillo

Confronting the Revolution

When one suffers from a situation and the given means of resolving it are objectionable, it is the duty of the individual to observe and analyze the correct ways of solving the problem.

As I said before, the first to understand the problem are not the very victims of the situation, but visionaries who confront it objectively, unhampered by its pressures.

I want to emphasize something: if a group of individuals is suffering from an intolerable, violent situation, then all of us must come to grips with their reality: some to face it out of honesty and human shame, and others to overcome it.

The individual must not remain stuck in fruitless analysis of the situation; the analysis should serve to bring about a theoretical understanding of the problem and, then, he must act on the theory. Being fully conscious of the urgency to make a revolutionary leap, he must have the courage to come face to face with it. This step causes a whole range of conformists and pseudo-revolutionaries to falter. Many of them become alarmed. And only honest individuals, who are honest revolutionaries, overcome this. The demagogues who wish to be taken for revolutionaries disclose, in time, their total lack of conscience.

It is also worth mentioning that the comprehension of revolutionary reality usually comes first to a small group of individuals, and then gradually it penetrates every area.

Our arrival at the highest level of confrontation with revolutionary reality means we have taken it upon ourselves to pass through stages of profound confusions and doubts, difficulties which cannot be overcome except by the force of conviction.

Even after facing up to revolutionary reality, many still are not oriented towards it. They are bound by lover's knots and family ties. They don't understand that commitment is the backbone of a determined generation. If the revolution calls on them to leave their loved ones and families, then the revolutionary must do so for the sake of a just cause.

There is a whole other group of individuals: those who have come face to face with revolutionary reality, but are incapable of actively engaging it. There is no method more shameful, no lie more premeditated.

> The cripples work,
> those with one arm work
> no one is useless, or out of work.
> The blind are employed shucking corn
> the children chasing birds.
>
> —Ernesto Cardenal

The Individual's Duty Toward The Revolution

The need for revolution comes of dangerous situations. If the individual has confronted revolutionary reality, then he has the obligation to actively engage that reality.

The individual is, first and foremost, a social being. Therefore, we have to present the case of Latin America as a block, as one union. We, the members of this generation, have one sole aim, one single column to form. We also have the blood that illuminates our rough footsteps: the blood of our older brother SAINT ERNESTO CHE GUEVARA. We are the generation obligated by our understanding of the situation.

There will be obstacles in the way of our march. In the first place, there is that banal urge to want TO LIVE ONE MINUTE MORE JUST TO LIVE, WITHOUT REALIZING THAT IF WE DON'T RELATE OUR ACTIONS TO THE LIBERATION OF THE PEOPLE, WHAT WE ARE MOSTLY DOING IS CONDEMNING THE PEOPLE WHO ARE INNOCENT.

The very fear of giving ourselves over to a life of sacrifice and an authentic revolutionary calling is what makes us fall into the most fatal conformism. We must not hope that the situation will somehow solve itself, overnight, without us doing our part. We must not wait for nor expect others to solve it for us.

We still don't understand that the total giving of our lives to the liberation of the people represents our DEATH, but with it we give LIFE. The duty of the revolutionary is to make revolution, without savoring the idea of seeing the triumph.

"The revolution is communion with the species."

Sweet wishful thinking about the future must not keep us from realizing our revolutionary ideal. Our mission is incommensurably human, and is, therefore, more important than any other mission.

The Student's Duty Toward The Revolution

In this section I am referring to students who have gone past the second level of education, that is to say, to UNIVERSITY STUDENTS, most of whom are mature and reasonably stable. From the moment one sets foot in the University, a serious commitment is being made. I wish to analyse this privileged group and its role in society.

Though the student has a theoretical vision of the situation, his understanding of it is limited. Therefore, he must live for a time among the oppressed class and, in this way, come to understand their problems. After completing this work, he must ask himself: what are the causes of exploitation, and what are the solutions? Peaceful revolution doesn't solve anything. Pacifism calls for a level of culture our people do not yet possess. In a country where there is so much ignorance, the victims can do little. Taking all these considerations into account, the student must arrive at the honest conclusion: "We are deeply to blame for each person who starves. We are responsible for each person who commits a crime. We are responsible for every wrongdoing and for each one in particular." And the universe will call down justice on us while we howl like anguished dogs. If the solution to the problem is within our grasp and we do not act upon it, we are more devastating than typhus or the plague.

The student has the obligation to arouse the oppressed masses and to show them the path to their own liberation. If I don't fulfill my obligation exactly as is indicated, I am a murderer, I am the only murderer, because the fact that there may be some of us who are knowledgeable about the problem, by itself, doesn't go to justify my offense. "I am the only murderer of the masses."

Therefore, the student must commit himself to an organization that is clearly revolutionary. Once this commitment is made, he must be vigilant and carry out the work that must be done. It is of utmost importance that the revolutionary-student study the methods other peoples have employed to win their freedom and, in this way, begin to develop a correct method based in and stemming out of our own material conditions and immediate situation.

There will be times when the organization calls on the student to abandon his studies and to dedicate himself completely to revolutionary activity. And his response to that call will be a barometer that measures the degree to which he is truly a revolutionary.

If, in the work that we carry out among the masses for their own liberation, our own life is needed, let's sow that life without expecting to be mentioned in the history of future generations. But let's be sure that our bones are the backbone of that history.

Leonel Rugama
Estelí, Nicaragua 1968

AFTERWORD

Doris María Tijerino, a Sandinista guerrilla leader, joined the FSLN in the mid-1960's. The following reminiscences are from the book *Doris Tijerino: inside the Nicaraguan Revolution,* by Margaret Randall, who interviewed her in exile in 1975.

I met Leonel in 1968. At the time I didn't know he was Leonel Rugama. We met at a house where he came to do some target shooting, some military exercises. My comrade, Ricardo, pointed out that Leonel—who had terrible eyesight, and wore glasses— had excellent aim. Later I met him at another safe house, and remembered him as the one who had such good aim.

Back then I was reading a book of poems by César Vallejo and Leonel talked to me about Vallejo, and we began to discuss Vallejo's poetry and some essays. . .after that he came every weekend, and we'd discuss literature.

Leonel loved to hear folk tales, stories of the people, and always wanted to know stories told in the countryside. He asked me to tell him about my childhood, and what games I played. I told him that they used to tell us there was a goblin in the house, a good goblin who brought us presents—when it was really my mother or my grandmother putting sweets in different places throughout the house as a surprise for us. . .and when I told this to Leonel, he said that in his house they were so poor that there weren't any good goblins. Just mean goblins, who threw stones, or goblins who hid the toys that he'd made himself out of broken pieces of wood and tin cans.

Leonel was a very simple person and at the same time amazing. Nobody who talked with him could imagine that he was Leonel Rugama, the writer of the essay "The Student and Revolution," that had won a prize in 1968 in a competition honoring comrade Casimiro Sotelo, when Leonel was just in his first year at the University. Much less could you imagine that he was the author of the poem, "The Earth Is A Satellite Of The Moon."

. . .Leonel liked to be told dreams and he asked me to tell him mine. When I told him I dreamt in color, he laughed and said that was because I had a happy childhood and that most of the people in the country dreamed in black and white. He said dreaming was like going to the movies: the most expensive movies were in color and the cheapest in black and white. Leonel told me he had had only one dream in his life—and that it had been in black and white.

. . .Even when the Guard came and assassinated Leonel, even then he was amazing. The way he answered the Guard!

We will keep on struggling. So someday all our people will dream in color.

I am René Espronceda de la Barca

to Doris (María Tijerino Haslam),
great admirer of César Vallejo.

In general, I never got through a difficult and challenging school assignment without doing a lot of work, and the more complex and intricate the readings were, on all sorts of subjects, the more I threw myself into it (—René, know what's playing at the movies today? René, don't you know what's playing at the movies today? I wanted to go, but I didn't have the time, and Silvia told me it's a beautiful movie, that it's one of the best films with Manrique Canal and Grieta Pardo, and also Parles Geton, Ticher Burlon and Sortija Flores are in it—), and I knew how to come up with smart answers, since it didn't matter if it rained or thundered, if they talked about me or not, if it was hot or cold, if it was wet or dry out, or if it was sunny or cloudy, or if the day started out soaked in rum or scorched by the sun, or if the rainy season never ended or it had subsided, or if the sky started to clear or if we were in Indian Summer, or if the girl who drinks chocolate milk came by or not, or if there were huge windstorms like when the devil boldly walks around during Easter Week, or wild blustery winds or gentle breezes, or sudden downpours, or endless rains that washed the streets clean, or if hail fell or fishes, the way they once fell on the doorsteps (also around Easter Week) and my uncle used to go around picking them up, sunfish and catfish—that's what they loved to call them—almost always rained down.

Or the World News blaring on the radio and all day long the soap operas or the year's top ten on the *hit* parade with singers singing full-volume, and the kids playing and racing their little cars and screaming as though their throats were going to burst, or if our neighbor's radio was on a different station, also turned way up, or if our neighbor on the left had tuned in his short-wave to Radio Havana and it's also blasting and the broadcaster is giving the news about the sugar harvests or the latest kidnapping or about the next amateur boxing championship or Fidel talking and giving a speech about intellectuals or the Second Havana Declaration, or "liberation movements will not disappear, for as long as there are people who are exploited, there will be men who bravely know how to grasp a gun" and all the transistor radios blaring and in the kitchen Argentina is washing the plates and the plates are banging against each other, or she's washing the spoons and the spoons are clanging against each other, and the noisy scouring brush or the toilet just flushed, or the rice sizzling or the beans bubbling or the coffee boiling, or the clothes being washed and scrubbed and pounded against the washboard and the sound of the water pouring off like a waterfall or rapids, or the sound of the soapy suds girgling down the drain and more noise when it occurs to Argentina to sing.

And the noise from a big truck going by, raising a big cloud of dust and the dust flying all over the place and getting all over the house and dirtying all the furniture and my clothes, and my shirt collar is filthy and so are the sleeves and kid's clothes, and Argentina sweeping the dust and raising another cloud of dust and the raspy voice of doña Joaquina telling her that it's better to spread wet sawdust on the floor because it keeps the dust down better and while she says this she sneezes and then Argentina sneezes and Argentina sneezes again and she saying, "Damn, I'm allergic to dust, but René apparently doesn't notice anything when he's wrapped up in his reading."

Or the Coca-Cola truck making a big racket with all the purple Fanta bottles and all the clear red Milca bottles rattling and fizzing up, or the ting-ling-a-ling-a-ling of a man who's selling ices or a man yelling 'Snowcones! Snowcones! Snowcones!' and the scraper scraping the ice to make the snowcones and then he says 'Here you are' and the squeaky wheels of all the carts and wagons, and the peddlers yelling 'Fresh vegetables! Fresh vegetables! Fresh vegetables!' and another 'Coal! Coal! Coal!' 'Firewood! Firewood!' 'Popcorn!' 'Bread!' 'La Preeeeeeensa! La Preeeeeeeeeensa! La Preeeeeeeeeeeeeeeeeeeensa!' 'Shellfish!' 'Pork! Pork! Pork!' and the ting-a-ling-a-ling-a-ling-a- ling-a-ling of a man who's selling fresh fruit with milk and containers of chocolate milk, and the 'you son-of-a-bitch' of one boy towards the other, and 'your mutha' 'she's yours' 'the old bitch' 'that lame-brain' 'the one who throws away tortillas' 'that fat slob' 'cheat' 'you know who' and the voices fade away little by little each one going their separate way.

Or the sound of a boy who goes by scratching the wall with a stick and from time to time stopping and writing 'asshole' 'pussy' 'prick' 'faggot' and he continues moving on, scratching the wall with his stick and shouting 'Drop dead you ugly bastards! Drop dead you ugly bastards! All of you, all of you, all you ugly bastards! Me, me, me. . .' and it would fade away and then one more time the shouting and the scratching on the wall.

Or two boys walking down the street and shouting and tossing a ball to each other and the bargain-seller barking 'Exciting! Dynamic! Exciting! dance for the benefit of Jesus the Crucified' or 'Big raffle for a luxury car for the benefit of the Consecrated Tomb' or 'Attention ladies and gentlemen! Attention ladies and gentlemen! We are here to let you have for the ridiculous sum of one small peso, for one córdoba, listen up good to this offer we're making for the ridiculous sum of one córdoba, one small peso, a peso, that's all, one single peso is next to nothing, you sir, you madam, you young man can take this marvelous, yes sir, yes madam, yes young lady, you can take this incredibly marvelous and cheap set of kitchen spoons for the ridiculous sum of. . .and here comes a nice young girl, yes, fine, and for one small peso the young lady has decided to take this marvelous and necessary set of spoons, you too sir, madam you as as well, you also young man can decide for yourself and stick to it, for the lousy sum of one peso, one córdoba, now that's not sky-high, one little peso doesn't make you rich, doesn't make you poor, yes young man, what will you have? What can we get you? Good, now he's getting away with only paying one córdoba national currency for this marvelous wonderful set of kitchen spoons, attention! attention ladies! attention ladies..!' and the loud noise from a motor bike that zips by backfiring and leaving a big cloud of smoke behind or the longslowanguishing sound of a bleedingredracingambulance or the squealing of a car peeling away fast and whipping around the corner like a gangster or the same car slamming on the brakes to let Jorge's son cross who's chasing after his ball and he's only a little shaken up, but if something had happened to the kid, Jorge would've gone nuts because he's always drunk and doesn't notice, and the one thing about Jorge is he loves his sons and whoever doesn't like it has to face him, and he's the kind of guy who. . .I remember when he (Jorge) kicked a servant just because she gave Roger (when he was little) a tiny scratch, and that was on her kneecap.

Or the noises sounding very far off and the kids in the square giving the woman who's always screaming at them a hard time. And not all the transistor radios blasting, not all the kids shouting and yelling, not all the trucks, not all the street peddlers and not even Argentina's grating voice can pull me away from my *fascinating* readings "The Truth about Dogmatic Theology" "A Year by Year History of the Development of Industrial Metaphysics" "Commentaries about a Trip Beyond the Grave" "The Most Famous Crimes" "Damned to Distrust" "The Folly of Eulogies" "Sand in the Blood" "The Rebirth of St. Francis of Assisi" "A Powerful Group of Theologians Congratulate God on His Naming" "The Death of Jesus with an Epilogue and Appendix of the Stages of the Cross" "An Atheist Contends That There Are Three Different People And One True God" "The Almighty" (authorized by the Holy Father of the Church of Leon XIII) "The Song of Songs" "The Martyr of the Segovias" "The Way of the Cross" "The Ultimate Magic of the Word" "Astrology" "The Divine Oracle" "The Problem of the Birth Rate and its Repercussions on the Last Judgment" "The Magnificant Prophecies of the Virtuous San Malaquías" these titles are in my latest notes on what I'm reading, that's right, and I remember I've read some other things and it all adds up to about twenty thousand famous biographies and close to five thousand famous poems and various 2nd-hand anthologies of the most famous poets in the history of the world, and the complete works of the theatre, leatherbound, and written on very delicate onion-skin paper. And on top of all this, I always keep up with the great source of information in the newspapers, paying principal attention to the literary and cultural pages.

Moreover, I must confess I cultivate the letters in my free time, devoting myself to composing the most finely honed verses, and not all the pandemonium in the world can get in the way of this work.

But today, after two months of being separated from Argentina, who left with all the kids because of certain extremely private problems, today I find myself totally cut-off—or at least in good part cut-off—from the maddening noise of the city which I find bearable, but here in one of the most isolated barrios in the city, here I'm beginning to go crazy in places where the silence is almost profound, which is an excellent quality but I don't need it, and it's not unbearable either due to my large capacity for adapting, that's right, at this very moment I'm beginning to go crazy, slowly, little by little, and then all of a sudden I go nuts without even time to wonder where my agony is leading, or if my craziness will be peaceful and if all the volunteers in the barrio will take care of me or if, on the contrary, I'll be a wild madman posing a big threat to the neighbors and if I'll decide at any minute to throw rocks at the front doors of all the houses or at the churches which is much worse, or if it dawns on me to take a bath and I don't come out till the Judgment Day, or, still worse, if I go to the john and sit there for a long time and nothing happens and I leave as satified as though I had done something, or I decide to tie my shoe-laces in knots so tight no one will ever be able to get them out, and I go walking around here with them like that till I drop from exhaustion or I wear down the heels and even the soles, walking around strung-out, on the edge, in knots (of course, I mean the shoes) or else never opening my mouth, not to eat or anything and spending year after year like that or poking my eyes out and staring at everybody with empty sockets and spitting at the first guy who makes a wise-crack; but something I've always been afraid of is going outside naked in the street, and stark naked like that all the folks in the barrio tie me up and bring me to the madhouse under the pretext that I'm crazy, that I've lost my grip or I've sprung a leak and then, even worse, they leave me there among so many strange nuts, when you don't know who they are, much less where they're from or what they're like, if they can take a joke; and actually what I'm scared of more than being tied up or brought to the madhouse or finding myself among so many strange nuts, is that they leave me in that house, the one I hate so much, because ever since I was little I sang in the church choir and always I wanted to throw something from the altar, because there was a strong angry odor and a stench of unbearable shit up there that was mixed with the foul smell of the crazies and some old withered flowers that they had placed on the altar.

Well, tonight I just barely started reading the newspaper when a fly wouldn't let me have any peace, and when I was reading 'an unfamiliar but always present page by Vallejo' the fly again landed on my head as though it was licking my hair, and I threatened it with the newspaper and it took off towards the candle "THE INTELLECTUALS (again I feel the fly on my head and I'm ready to give it a good swat and again it flies off towards the candle) AND POLITICS."

The artist is, unavoidably, a political person. His lack of purpose, his lack of political sensibility, should serve to demonstrate spiritual barrenness, human mediocrity, and aesthetic inferiority. But, within this setting, must the artist become politically active? His field of political action is multiple: he can vote, he can protest, such as leading a group of civic-minded people, like from any barrio (and now the fly is buzzing around my ear and flying around my head and buzzing around my ear again, and now worse, it landed on my ear and has started to walk around in there, well, a good whack ended that and now it's circling the candle and I can't see a thing from staring at the light, and it's driving me crazy and I'm starting to get a coughing attack and the fly manages to land on my neck and is walking around my collar and the coughing's getting worse— enough already! and now I'm so afraid of spitting on the floor and this spit in my mouth pisses me off and the fly continues its trek across my back, and it bugs me, so to speak, when insects go for long hikes on your skin, so I sit up and try scratching my back when I notice that the fly is trapped in my shirt and this is a relief, because now I can decide the fate of this damn louse, and though I feel a little queasy I'm driven by necessity and the miserable time I'm having, so I try squashing it between my back and the chair—I think I got it, ugh! and I think I can get almost any disease from squashing an insect so full of germs), he can lead a doctrinal, national, continental, radical or universal movement along the lines of Rolland. In all these ways the artist can, certainly, serve in politics; but none of them answer to the powers of political creation—creating, by preference, inquietudes and political nebulas peculiar to his nature— and none of them end up being more than anyone's catechism or collection of formulated and, therefore, limited ideas (but if the same fly that I killed on my back is again on my hand, and worse, sucking me dry and leaving a wet ooze right where I hold my top, ugh! disgusting! and I already shooed it away but the damn fly came back and now it's dancing right in front of my eyes trying to get in them, and up my nose, and maybe I should just leave it alone and let it bother me, but it keeps chasing me and I feel the uncontrollable urge to cough and powerless to spit and that fly won't leave me in peace, and I wish I had two mad-dogs or *lagartija* lizards or *pichetes* (three different names and one true animal) so that the two of them would swallow it up in one gulp, and damn this coughing and I have to make myself get up to spit hawkers out in the backyard because of the same stupid fear of spitting on the sidewalks just because it's not my house, and the fly lands on my head, on my foot, on my hand, on my back, on my face, on my ear and it tries going up my nose, in my ear, in my mouth, flying buzzing around, around my head wanting to land on my mouth on my eyes again trying to get in my mouth again going for long walks across my back, shitting on my tongue, walking around in my lungs, nesting in my stomach, buzzing buzzing buzzing, walking on my face on my mouth on my nose) if the artist gives up creating what we could call the political nebula radiating throughout human nature—reducing it with propaganda and proclamations from the barricade itself to a secondary, sporadic sun—who then would be touched by that great and wondrous spirit in all of us?

—Leonel Rugama